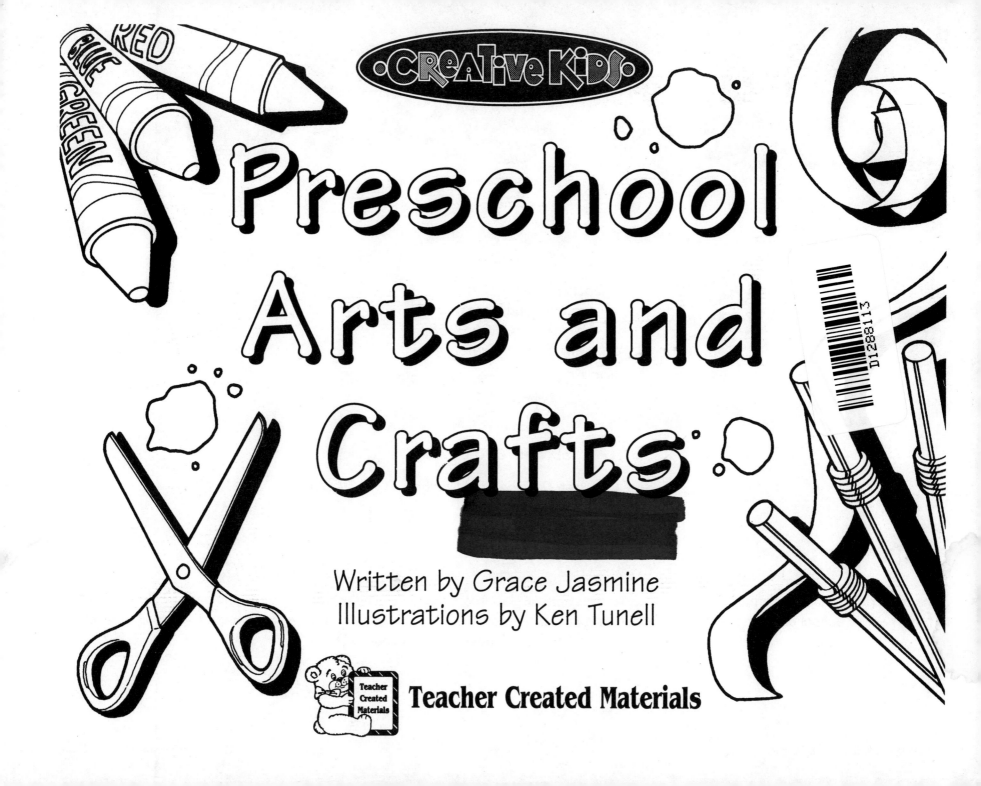

Creative Kids

Preschool Arts and Crafts

Written by Grace Jasmine

Illustrations by Ken Tunell

Teacher Created Materials

Teacher Created Materials, Inc.
6421 Industry Way
Westminster, CA 92683
www.teachercreated.com

© 1997 Teacher Created Materials, Inc.
Reprinted, 2001

Made in U.S.A.

ISBN-1-57690-097-5

Library of Congress Catalog Card Number: 96-061506

Editor:
Janet Cain

Table of Contents

Table of Contents *(cont.)*

Introduction

Arts and Crafts at Home with Your Preschooler

<u>Preschool Arts and Crafts</u> is a 160-page book filled with poetry and fun ideas for arts and crafts activities. It was created for parents to use with their preschool children.

This book includes many types of projects that will appeal to preschoolers because young children love coloring and making arts and crafts projects. In addition, it provides them with opportunities to feel successful as they learn that there are many things they can do without your help.

Although these projects were compiled for children and parents, they can easily be adapted for the classroom. Teachers need only multiply the amount of materials by the number of students participating to have a new resource for arts and crafts activities that can be integrated into thematic units.

The activities in this book make use of materials that are easily obtained. Most of the items you probably already have in your home. Any items that you need to buy can be found in grocery, drug, art and craft, and/or teacher supply stores. Recycling can provide many of the items. For example, consider cleaning and saving a variety of empty food containers for future projects. In addition, some projects require materials that are found in nature. It is important to stress to children that they should collect natural things without harming the environment.

Expectations

You may be tempted to do things yourself, but be patient and remember that these are your child's creations. Contribute only what is necessary for your child to proceed, and be ready to rave about the results—no matter what they look like! Enjoy this creative time with your child.

Experts in the field of early childhood education favor "self-directed activities." This means that they feel it is very important for young children to be able to do things for themselves. As you let your child become more self-directed, keep in mind the following:

- The arts and crafts experiences will not always go as planned. In fact, this book is designed to allow children to explore their own ideas.

- Sometimes there will be a mess to clean up. Invite your child to help you clean up and put away materials.

- Your child might get frustrated and need some additional help and guidance from you.

- You will need to prepare ahead of time. See How to Use This Book (page 7) for preparation suggestions.

- You will need to be available to help your child. Although this book was designed to provide the kinds of activities that preschoolers can do by themselves, you should never leave your child unsupervised. It is essential that you are there to ensure safety, give help when needed, and provide encouragement.

- As your child has more practice doing arts and crafts, his or her skill level will increase dramatically in some areas.

- Be sure to listen to your child's preferences for the types of activities he or she enjoys most.

Introduction *(cont.)*

Getting Started

The projects in this book can be done in any order and can be changed in any way to suit your needs. Help your child get started by reading aloud the directions and talking about the project. Be sure to check the "Kid Kit" pages to ensure you have the materials that are necessary for the projects before your child begins working.

Poetry and Your Preschooler

A unique feature of <u>Preschool Arts and Crafts</u> is the use of relevant poetry throughout the book. Each activity includes an original children's poem that will give you an additional opportunity to read aloud to your child and a wonderful way for you to talk about different ideas that are both related to the activity at hand and of interest to your child.

Before beginning any activity you might choose to read the corresponding poem. However, you may prefer to read the poems at your child's bedtime or any other quiet sharing time. It is up to you and your child to decide when you would most enjoy using the poetry in this book.

Why Is Poetry Important?

Poetry is important for your child at an early age, because the fun and entertaining use of language and rhyme helps him or her develop the cognitive thinking skills that are needed throughout life. Additionally, reading poetry to your child will build his or her vocabulary and provide pre-reading skills that he or she will need when starting school. Poetry will broaden your child's outlook and provide opportunities to see the world in many different ways. It is important to recognize that any reading you do with your child promotes his or her literacy.

How to Use the Poetry in this Book

Use the poems in this book as part of a regular reading time and as an opportunity to converse with your child. When you read a poem about a specific subject, ask your child what he or she knows or thinks about it and how he or she feels about it. By doing so, you are developing excellent communication with your child at an early age.

How to Use This Book

"Kid Kits"

Before using the projects in this book, look at each section and the corresponding "Kid Kit" page. This page will help you prepare for a specific kind of activity so that you have a whole set of arts and crafts experiences at your fingertips ready for your child to explore. Each activity has a corresponding original poem to get your child thinking and excited about the theme of that activity whether the poem is read before, during, or after the project.

Organizing the "Kid Kits"

When you are attempting to do arts and crafts projects at home with your preschooler, it often seems exhausting before you even start. This is why the ideas in this book all fit into a "Kid Kit" format.

The arts and crafts experiences have been divided into sections for which you put together a "Kid Kit." In this kit, you should place all of the materials needed for the section with the exception of those that can spoil or that are unusual. This way you will only have to prepare once for each section. You may wish to include other materials in the kit that relate to each section for activities that you devise for your child.

Your completed "Kid Kits" can be stored and used again and again. In addition, these kits provide you with a place to put everything away, a vital part of doing arts and crafts with a preschooler.

Preparing the "Kid Kits"

For your "Kid Kits," use large cardboard boxes with lids, such as those used for storing files or copier paper. Other options include large rectangular laundry hampers with lids or large plastic containers that can be found in the storage or housewares section of home improvement or hardware stores. Make sure each box can be labeled and that the lid can be placed securely on it.

Materials for the "Kid Kits"

Look through the book and decide which kits you are interested in putting together first. For a number of them, you may have many or most of the materials on hand. For some, you may need to make, recycle, or buy things.

Look at the activities that are included in each section and find the ones that you know will appeal to your child the most, based on her or his skill level and interests. Then put the kit together. You may wish to reproduce the "Kid Kit" list and tape it to the lid of the box. This way you can easily determine what belongs in the kit and see that those materials are replaced after each use.

Once you have the kit put together, you do not have to run around doing everything for your child, so she or he can have an arts and crafts experience. You are free to facilitate the activities and let your child complete them in a much more self-directed way.

Storing the "Kid Kits"

Clean out an upper shelf of a closet for kit storage. Make sure that you supervise the use of each kit with your preschooler. An upper shelf is a perfect place to keep the kits out of the way until you are ready to use one with your child.

Fun Ways to Display Art

Art Galleries Everywhere!

It is easy to make an at-home art gallery, practically anywhere in your home. Your preschooler will love to see her or his art displayed and enjoyed by you and other family members. The following are several quick and easy art gallery ideas that can be done in an instant.

Refrigerator Art Gallery

Just buy a package of refrigerator magnets, and you are ready to begin displaying your preschooler's projects. Make sure you have enough magnets for your child to put one on each of the four corners of her or his creation. Stores often sell these refrigerator magnets at inexpensive prices. Buy a number of them so it will be possible to hang as many pictures as you have space for on your refrigerator. Let your child be in charge of hanging her or his own artwork in this easy-to-use, no-mess, no-fuss way!

Wall Art Gallery

There are many ways to hang art on your walls without damaging them. One way is to use tiny gift wrapping bows to attach the pictures to the wall. These bows will usually hold up the pictures without removing the paint from the wall. Also, they look very festive and can easily be manipulated by a young child.

Bulletin Board Art Gallery

Any bulletin board you have around your house can serve as an art gallery. Be sure it is visible to everyone in the family and that you frequently change the display. A bulletin board allows you to use staples to affix the larger, heavier projects.

For a bulletin board that is placed within reach of a toddler, make sure to completely supervise the use of thumbtacks or pins. In most cases, you will probably not want to use them at all. It is usually better to staple the art to the bulletin board since little fingers cannot easily remove the staples.

Door Gallery

Some children enjoy displaying their projects on the back of their bedroom doors; however, any door in the house can be used for this type of gallery. You may wish to wrap the door with butcher paper or wrapping paper to provide a colorful background for your child's creations.

Safety First

Remember to use common sense about safety with your preschooler at all times. A brief reminder of safety rules as they relate to the arts and crafts activities in this book include the following:

- Before assembling "Kid Kits," check all purchased supplies for the label "non-toxic."

- Check your child's work area for safety. Make sure that all outlets are covered with safety covers, and that all dangerous or fragile objects are removed.

- Supervise the use of small objects and stress that they are never to be put in or near your child's mouth.

- Keep materials out of reach when not in use. Store "Kid Kits" on a closet shelf between activities.

- Wash egg shells thoroughly to prevent contamination. Add a tiny amount of chlorine bleach to the cleaning water to kill bacteria. Keep this procedure away from children.

- Use a plastic tablecloth to protect work surfaces and tables.

- Talk with your child about safety concerns as you go along. It is never too early to begin to communicate about safety.

- Remove all sharp objects from your child's work area.

- Remember, common sense prevents most accidents.

Drawing, Cutting, and Pasting

"Kid Kit"

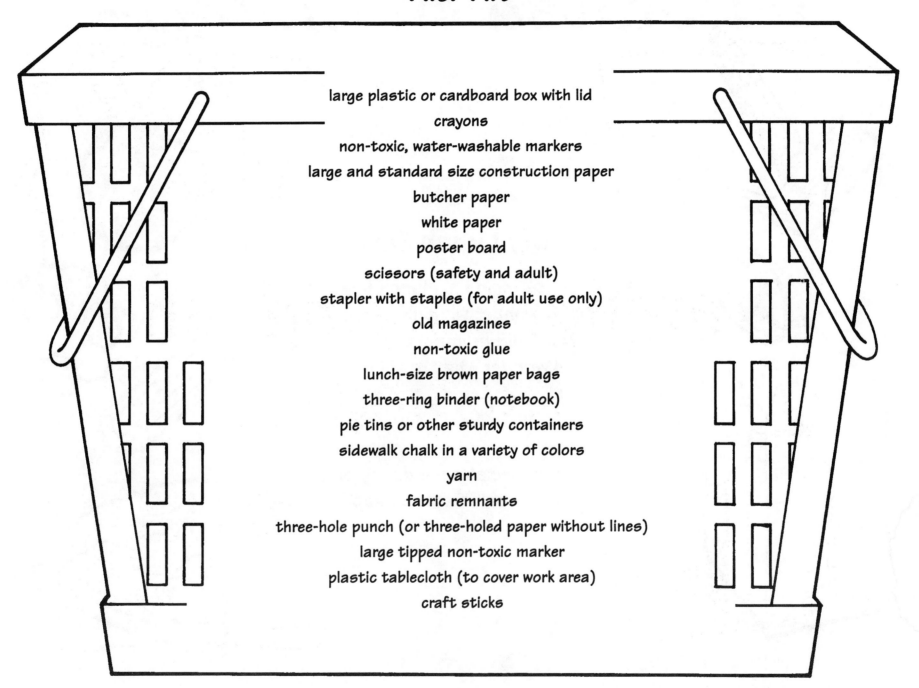

large plastic or cardboard box with lid

crayons

non-toxic, water-washable markers

large and standard size construction paper

butcher paper

white paper

poster board

scissors (safety and adult)

stapler with staples (for adult use only)

old magazines

non-toxic glue

lunch-size brown paper bags

three-ring binder (notebook)

pie tins or other sturdy containers

sidewalk chalk in a variety of colors

yarn

fabric remnants

three-hole punch (or three-holed paper without lines)

large tipped non-toxic marker

plastic tablecloth (to cover work area)

craft sticks

#2097 Preschool Arts and Crafts

Decorated Lunch Bags

My Lunch Bag

I look inside my lunch bag.
I wonder what I'll see,
What did mommy pack me?
I wonder what it will be.

It might be a sandwich,
Some fruit and a special treat.
I wonder what's inside my bag.
I just can't wait to eat!

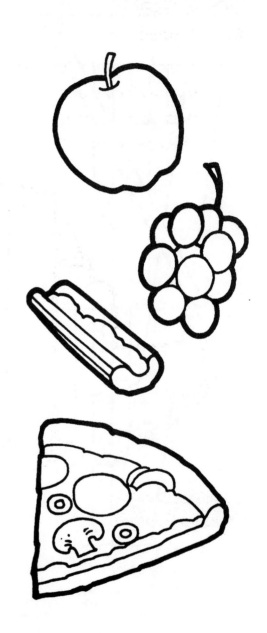

Decorated Lunch Bags

Ready!

You will need:

- lunch-size brown paper bags,
- crayons or markers
- construction paper
- safety scissors
- non-toxic glue

Set, Go!

This activity is an easy one that every child will love. All that is needed are crayons and brown paper bags and your child can decorate his own bags for lunch or snack. Make it a weekend activity to create bags for the following week.

Suggest that your child draw pictures of the family, flowers, shapes, dots, lines, or anything else that he would like.

Another idea is to provide scissors, construction paper, and non-toxic glue for your child to cut and paste shapes and designs on the bags.

Remember!

This is an activity that can be used almost anytime and anywhere. Something that makes it extra special is that children can really use the bags for their own preschool snacks or school lunches.

Another idea is to add ribbons and bows to the colored and decorated bags and use them for wrapping small gifts.

ABC Cut and Glue Pictures

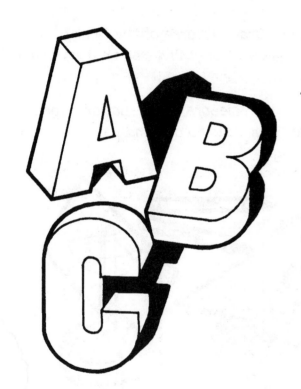

My ABC's

Look at all the letters!
They are the ABC's.
The letters make the words we read
As easy as can be!

When I'm a little older,
I'll learn how to read,
And the way that I'll get started is
To learn my ABC's!

a, b, c, d, e, f, g,
h, i, j, k, l, m, n, o, p,
q, r, s, t, u, v,
w, x, y, z

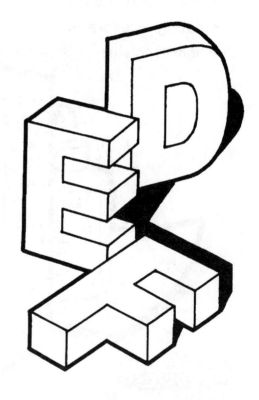

ABC Cut and Glue Pictures

Ready!

You will need:

- old magazines
- large piece of construction paper or poster board
- safety scissors
- non-toxic glue
- markers
- crayons

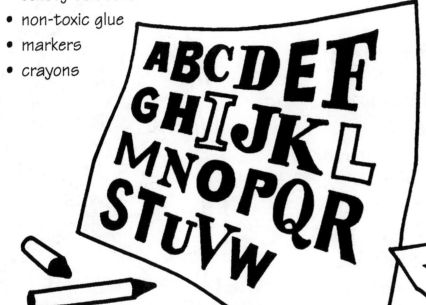

Set, Go!

To prepare for this activity, write the alphabet in large letters on a large piece of construction paper or poster board. If your child can do this, let her.

Then provide your child with safety scissors and a variety of old magazines, so she can cut out the letters of the alphabet. Children's magazines work especially well because they usually have large, child-friendly letters that are easier to cut out. If you do not have any magazines, newspapers may be substituted. All magazines and newspapers will have large, bold letters that will be fun for your child to cut out.

Provide non-toxic glue for your child to glue the letters onto the paper, and she will finish with an ABC picture!

Remember!

Depending on the interests and skill level of your child, she may want to spell words with the letters or identify the letters of words that have been cut out.

You may wish to suggest that your child spell her own name from letters that are cut out. Provide assistance with the spelling of your child's name as needed.

Life-Size Self-Portrait

My Reflection

What do I look like?
What do I see?
When I look in the mirror,
I see me!

From the top of my head
To the tip of my toes,
I see the me
That everyone knows!

16

Life-Size Self-Portrait

You will need:

- butcher paper or poster board
- large tipped non-toxic marker
- crayons
- adult scissors
- non-toxic glue
- yarn
- fabric remnants

Remember!

Set, Go!

This activity is almost every young child's favorite. Just find a large space on the floor and have your child lie down on a large sheet of butcher paper or poster board. Then trace around your preschooler with a large tipped marker.

You may wish to give your child a variety of art materials to create his own self-portrait. However, it is possible for him to do the whole activity using only crayons. For an extra special life-size self-portrait, provide yarn for hair and fabric remnants for clothing.

For extra fun, switch places and let your child trace your form on butcher paper, and then draw and decorate your portrait.

Cut out each portrait and hang the finished products on your bedroom doors or tape them to the inside of a window, so your family portraits can "watch" you leave and come home each day.

My Family Picture Book

My Family

I have a family.
I love them. Yes, I do.
We belong together,
And I know they love me too!

The people in my family,
They belong to me.
And we are all a part of
The same family tree!

(Name the people in your family with your child.)

My Family Picture Book

You will need:

- white paper
- three-ring binder (notebook)
- three-hole punch (or three-holed paper without lines)
- crayons
- markers
- photographs of family members (optional)

Set, Go!

Tell your child that she will use the binder (notebook) and paper to make a special book that can be added to again and again. This kind of notebook can also serve as a treasured keepsake for storing your child's drawing.

Explain to your child that she can make a family picture book. Most children will enjoy drawing family members they see every day. However, if your child has other relatives, such as grandparents, uncles, aunts, and cousins that she does not see very often, this is an excellent time to share their pictures and explain who these relatives are. This step is optional.

Below each picture of a family member, help your child write the name of that person.

As your child creates pictures of the family, punch holes in each paper and place the drawings in the notebook. Your child will have a notebook that she will enjoy looking at and "reading."

Remember!

Family members will love to see their portraits, so remember to share.

To save time and extra work, you can purchase pre-punched blank white paper at drug or stationary stores.

Magazine Match

Pictures

I love to look at pictures.
I can see so many things,
Like cats, and dogs, and bicycles,
Like playgrounds with slides and swings.

I love to look at pictures.
I see places I've never been.
Places I might go one day.
Oh, how I wonder when!

Magazine Match

You will need:

- old magazines
- construction paper
- non-toxic glue
- pie tins or other sturdy containers
- craft sticks
- crayons or markers
- safety scissors

This activity will keep your preschooler entertained for a long period of time. Make Magazine Match pages ahead of time by selecting four interesting and simple pictures.

Then fold a piece of construction paper to make eight boxes. Hold the paper vertically so that there are two columns of four boxes each. Glue the magazine pictures in the boxes on the left side. Your child can then draw the same picture in the boxes on the right side.

To make this a more in-depth activity, your child can also select the pictures, cut them out, and glue them on the paper before making the drawings. Put a small amount of glue into a pie tin or container and have your child use a craft stick to spread it. You can also extend this activity by using the boxes on the back of the construction paper.

Remember!

These Magazine Match activities can be prepared ahead of time and placed in your child's "Kid Kit" so that they are ready for those times when he needs something to do and you need some quiet time.

These activities are easy to carry or pack. Take them with you when you go on trips or visits in order to keep your child from getting bored.

Magazine Mural

I Can Do It By Myself!

I can do it by myself!
Each day I do much more.
Once when I was much too small,
I could not reach the door.

Now I put on both my shoes,
And even ride a trike.
I can do them by myself,
So many things I like!

I can even write my name,
And run and jump and play.
I can hop and I can skip,
There's more to do each day!

Magazine Mural

You will need:

- poster board or butcher paper
- non-toxic glue
- safety scissors
- old magazines
- pie tins or other sturdy containers
- craft sticks
- plastic tablecloth

Set, Go!

Provide lots of old magazines with colorful pictures, poster board, and glue, and your preschooler can make his own Magazine Mural.

With safety scissors, your child will be able to cut out the magazine pictures and then glue them to the posterboard or butcher paper. (Pour glue into a pie tin or container. Have your child use a craft stick to apply glue.) After the mural is finished, hang it on the wall in your child's bedroom for display.

Remember!

Use construction paper and your child can make placemats. Cover them with contact paper to make them more durable and easier to keep clean.

Chalk Drawing

Chalk Rainbow

Beautiful colors on the walk,
A wonderful rainbow of colorful chalk,
And when the rain comes down to play,
My wonderful rainbow will wash away!

And when the sun peeks from a cloud,
I'll laugh, and point, and shout aloud.
My wonderful rainbow that washed away
Is shimmering up in the sky today!

Chalk Drawing

You will need:

- outdoor sidewalk area
- sidewalk chalk in a variety of colors
- old play clothes

Drawing with chalk is a favorite for most preschool children. It is an easy, self-directed activity that will take a minimum of preparation. Just purchase sidewalk chalk which should be very inexpensive and readily available. Buy several packages so you never run out.

Find a place for your child to draw. If you do not have a sidewalk or cement area near your own home, most parks or playgrounds will have places where children are allowed to use sidewalk chalk since it washes off.

Have your child wear old play clothes because sidewalk drawing does get messy. Wearing clothes that can get dirty will give your child the freedom to enjoy the activity.

Remember!

Here are some interesting ways to get a child started:

Draw large hearts, squares, and circles for your child to draw pictures in or color.

Use chalk to trace an outline of your child. Then let your child draw himself.

Have your child draw with a friend.

Painting

26

"Kid Kit"

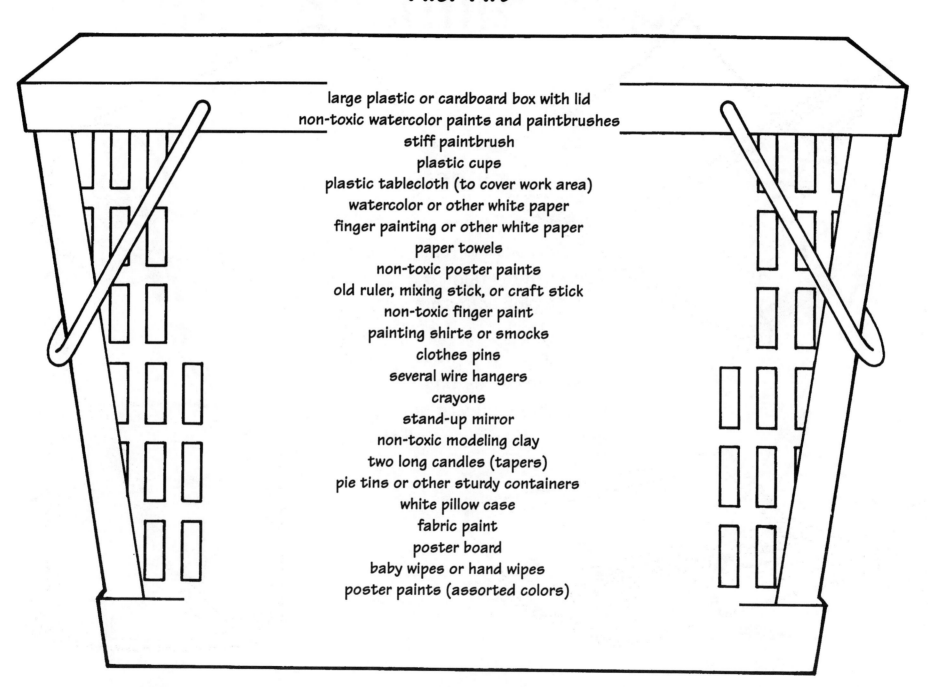

large plastic or cardboard box with lid
non-toxic watercolor paints and paintbrushes
stiff paintbrush
plastic cups
plastic tablecloth (to cover work area)
watercolor or other white paper
finger painting or other white paper
paper towels
non-toxic poster paints
old ruler, mixing stick, or craft stick
non-toxic finger paint
painting shirts or smocks
clothes pins
several wire hangers
crayons
stand-up mirror
non-toxic modeling clay
two long candles (tapers)
pie tins or other sturdy containers
white pillow case
fabric paint
poster board
baby wipes or hand wipes
poster paints (assorted colors)

Finger Painting Fun

Fingers

I have five fingers on each hand,
And that is really handy.
For when my fingers get to work,
I'll color something dandy.

I can paint a pretty picture,
And make my fingers "snap."
With handy fingers such as mine,
I can surely *do* all that!

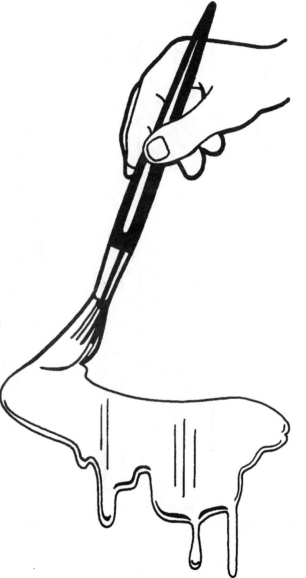

Finger Painting Fun

Ready!

You will need:

- plastic tablecloth
- finger painting or other white paper
- old clothes, paint shirt, or smock
- non-toxic finger paint
- clothes pins
- several wire hangers

Set, Go!

Cover a table with a plastic tablecloth. If the weather is nice, you may wish to move the activity outside.

Provide your child with one or several colors of finger paint. Make sure your child is wearing old clothes, a paint shirt, or a smock since finger painting is messy.

There is special finger painting paper that you can buy. However, you can also use any kind of white paper that has a smooth surface.

After your child's creation is complete, place it on a hanger using clothes pins. Allow the painting to dry.

Remember!

Before beginning, pick a place to hang the finger paintings while they are drying. This will make your clean-up easier.

Finger paintings make excellent wrapping paper too. Make sure the paintings are completely dry before pressing the paper under several large, heavy books.

Let your child finger paint on a regular basis so he can experiment with different colors.

Deep Blue Sea Picture

Goldfish Days

Goldfish, goldfish, in a bowl,
Are you out for a little stroll?
Swimming here and there today,
Through the seaweed and on your way.

You stop to talk to Mister Snail,
Who makes his way along his trail.
You tip your fin and swim away,
And that's what my goldfish did today!

Deep Blue Sea Picture

Ready!

You will need:

- non-toxic watercolor paints
- watercolor paintbrushes
- plastic cup
- water
- old ruler, mixing stick, or craft stick
- watercolor or other white paper
- crayons
- paper towels
- plastic tablecloth

Set, Go!

Have your child make an underwater picture using her crayons. Explain to your child that after the picture is done you will show her how to make it really special.

Make a blue watercolor wash by adding water to blue watercolor paint in a cup. Mix with an old ruler, mixing stick, or craft stick. The mixture should leave a blue tint when applied to the paper.

Let your child use a paintbrush to apply this blue watercolor wash over the picture. The crayon sections will not hold the watercolor, and the end result will be a wonderful "ocean" effect that your child will love.

Remember!

Make sure your child does not use crayon to color in the water parts of the picture since the blue wash will only tint the paper where there is no crayon.

Painting My Face

My Face

When I look into the mirror,
There is someone that I see,
Can you guess that person's name?
Yes, you're right, it's me!

My mother says my hair is nice.
My father likes my eyes.
And I admit I like myself,
And that is no surprise!

Painting My Face

You will need:

- watercolor or other white paper
- plastic tablecloth
- non-toxic watercolor paints
- watercolor paintbrush
- plastic cup
- water
- stand-up mirror

Set, Go!

Set up your child's painting area by covering a table with a plastic tablecloth and placing the mirror so your child can easily see his face.

Then provide watercolors, paper, and paintbrushes so your child can make a self-portrait by looking at his face in the mirror.

Make sure the watercolor painting is completely dry before moving it, so the paints will not run.

Remember!

This is an activity your child can try several times a year. Keep the results to compare them. Your child will be interested in how he painted herself at different ages. Also, these self-portraits make wonderful keepsakes for you.

Painted Candle Holders

Light a Candle

A candle, a candle,
Brightens the night,
A tiny beacon
Of golden light.

Light candles of goodness,
Every day,
So a friendly light,
Will brighten your way.

Painted Candle Holders

Ready!

You will need:

- plastic tablecloth
- non-toxic modeling clay
- poster paints (assorted colors)
- paintbrushes
- pie tins or other sturdy containers
- two long candles (tapers)

Set, Go!

Cover your child's work space with a plastic tablecloth and provide her with clay and different colored poster paints poured into pie tins.

Then show your child how to roll a ball of clay and push a candle into it. This will produce an amazingly easy-to-make candle holder.

Remove the candles and paint the candle holders.

Allow the paint to dry thoroughly before using the candles.

Remember!

These make wonderful gifts that your child can easily make for the whole family.

Provide holiday colors before various holidays so your child can make candle holders that fit the season.

Painted Object

Things

There are so many things 'round me,
I love to see them all.
They're things of wonder, sometimes big,
And then they're sometimes small.

Pictures, clocks, and windows, I see!
And sofas! Lamps! A chair!
So many things I see 'round me,
For things are everywhere!

Painted Object

You will need:

- plastic tablecloth
- paintbrushes
- old clothes, paint shirt, or smock
- any old object
- poster paints
- paper towels

Set, Go!

This activity is very simple, but children adore it!

Just find an old object that you no longer need and that is safe for your child to handle. This can be an old toy, a jewelry box, empty oatmeal containers or food boxes, or even an old door or piece of wood. Let your child paint the object you have chosen.

Children will enjoy this kind of painting for hours. The object can be reused many times by changing the color your child paints with. As simple as this activity sounds, it is something youngsters will enjoy doing again and again.

Remember!

Be sure to pick an object that does not have any small parts that will fall off so that it is safe for your child to paint.

Consider doing this activity in your garage or in another work area that is not inside your house.

Fabric Painted Pillow Case

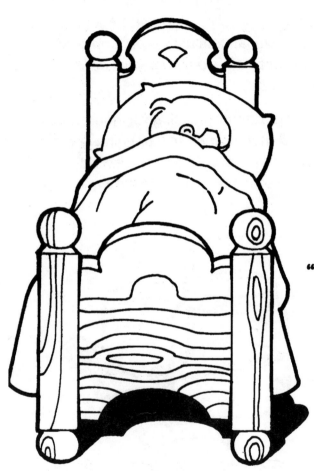

Goodnight

Goodnight, sleep tight,
It's time to go to bed.
Goodnight, sleep tight,
And rest your weary head.

The stars are shining bright.
The moon has come to say,
"It's time to go to Slumberland,
So let's be on our way."

Goodnight, sleep tight,
It's time to go to bed!
Goodnight, sleeptight,
Tomorrow lies ahead!

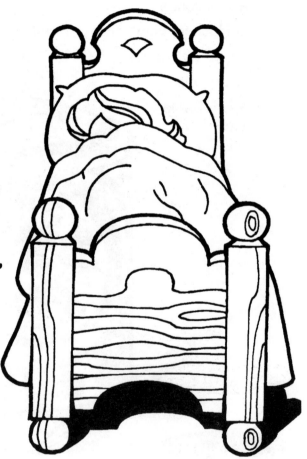

Fabric Painted Pillow Case

You will need:

- white pillow case
- non-toxic fabric paint
- stiff paintbrush
- poster board

Provide your child with a white pillow case and several kinds of fabric paint and let him decorate a pillow case.

Before your child begins painting, insert a piece of poster board or cardboard inside the pillow case so the pillow case layers will not stick together as the fabric paint is applied.

Allow the pillow case to dry thoroughly before using it. Launder according to the directions on the fabric paint.

These make unique and wonderful gifts.

To make the pillow case last longer, designate the painted case for use on a pillow that is for decoration and not for weary little heads.

For an interesting "designer" look, have your child make a set of these pillow cases using the colors found in his room.

Face Painting

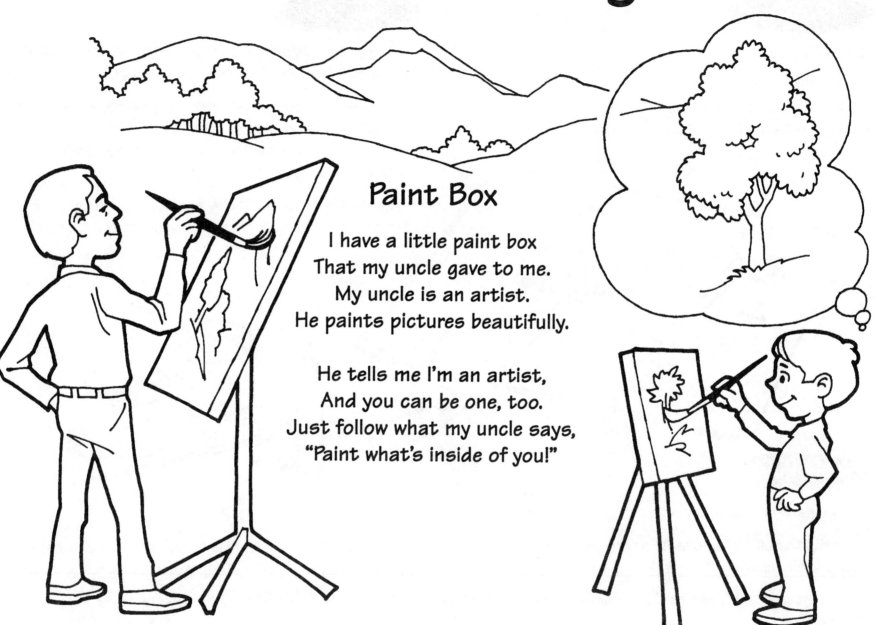

Paint Box

I have a little paint box
That my uncle gave to me.
My uncle is an artist.
He paints pictures beautifully.

He tells me I'm an artist,
And you can be one, too.
Just follow what my uncle says,
"Paint what's inside of you!"

Face Painting

You will need:

- plastic tablecloth
- stand-up mirror
- poster paints
- plastic cups
- old clothes
- small paintbrushes
- paper towels
- baby wipes or hand wipes

Set, Go!

This face-painting activity will amuse your child, but make sure he starts by putting on old clothes.

Mix several kinds of poster paint and place a stand-up mirror on the covered table so your child can easily see himself.

Then let your child paint his own face. Suggest some ideas, such as a Rudolph nose or a cat's whiskers, or let your child's imagination run wild.

This makes an interesting activity for a party and is best done outside.

Remember!

Poster paint is non-toxic and cannot harm your child. However, if your child has particularly sensitive skin, you may want to be extra cautious. To prevent injury to the face, supervise your child at all times.

Keep baby or hand wipes and paper towels on hand for clean up.

Kitchen Arts and Crafts

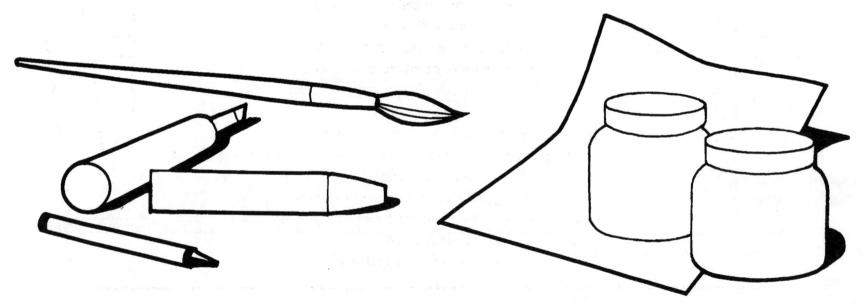

42

"Kid Kit"

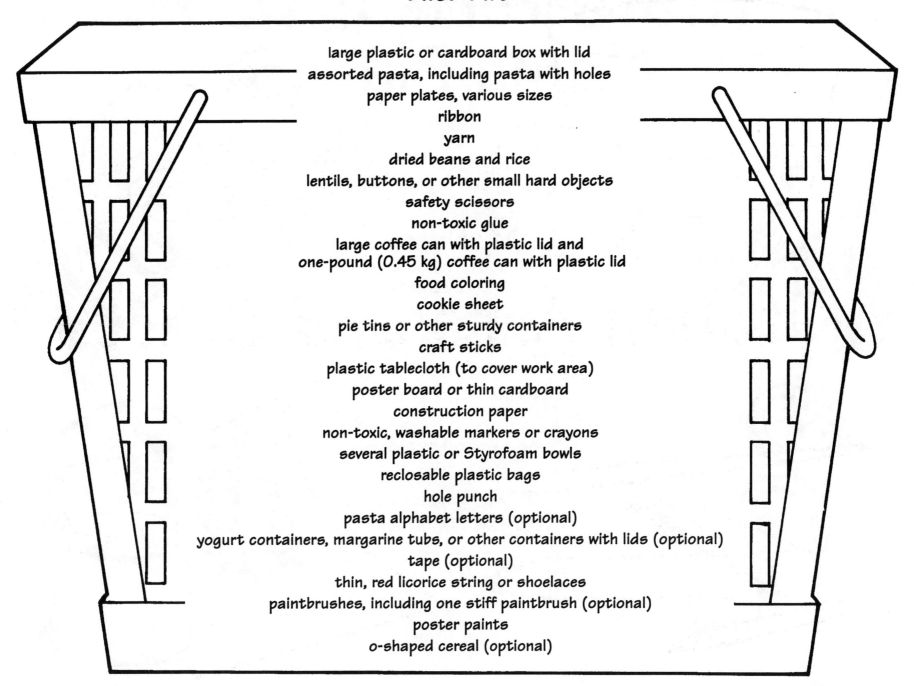

large plastic or cardboard box with lid

assorted pasta, including pasta with holes

paper plates, various sizes

ribbon

yarn

dried beans and rice

lentils, buttons, or other small hard objects

safety scissors

non-toxic glue

large coffee can with plastic lid and
one-pound (0.45 kg) coffee can with plastic lid

food coloring

cookie sheet

pie tins or other sturdy containers

craft sticks

plastic tablecloth (to cover work area)

poster board or thin cardboard

construction paper

non-toxic, washable markers or crayons

several plastic or Styrofoam bowls

reclosable plastic bags

hole punch

pasta alphabet letters (optional)

yogurt containers, margarine tubs, or other containers with lids (optional)

tape (optional)

thin, red licorice string or shoelaces

paintbrushes, including one stiff paintbrush (optional)

poster paints

o-shaped cereal (optional)

Pasta-Perfect Door Name Plates

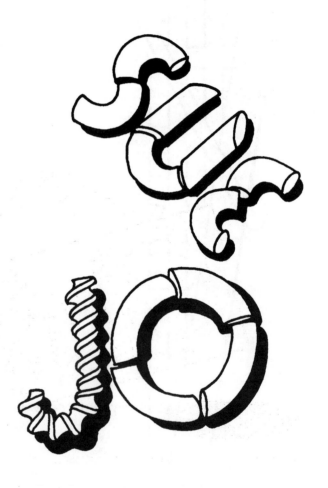

My Name

I love my name.
It makes me proud.
I love to say
My name aloud!
(Say your child's name.)

And when I'm older,
You will see,
I'll write my name
And say, "That's me!"

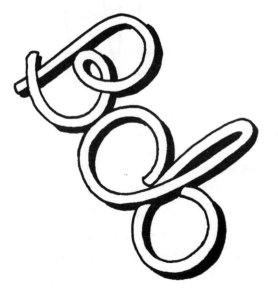

Pasta-Perfect Door Name Plates

Ready!

You will need:

- poster board or thin cardboard
- non-toxic glue
- assorted pasta
- ribbon
- safety scissors
- hole punch

Set, Go!

It is easy for your preschooler to make wonderful door name plates for every member of your family, even if she cannot spell.

Just give your child a piece of poster board or thin cardboard. Use glue to write your child's name or the name of another family member on the poster board or cardboard.

Have your child cover the glue with pasta, and she has made a wonderful name plate. Have her make a name plate for each family member.

Let the glue dry overnight. Help your child add bows tied from ribbon for extra decoration. Punch a hole on each side at the top of the name plates. Tie the ends of a piece of ribbon in the holes and hang each name plate on the wall or on each person's bedroom door.

Remember!

Talk with your child about his name and name the letters as you write them with the glue.

Try presenting other simple words. All you have to do is write them with the glue and have your child cover the glue with pasta.

Draw shapes with the glue and let your child cover these with pasta, too.

Pasta Plates

Circles

A circle is a shape I make.
It's round like this . . .
(Make a circle with your hands.)
Like a birthday cake!

I look so carefully to see
The circle shapes
Around me!

I see . . .
(Help your child name things that have circle shapes.)

Pasta Plates

You will need:

- paper plates
- ribbon
- assorted pasta
- non-toxic glue
- craft stick
- hole punch
- safety scissors
- food coloring (optional)
- reclosable plastic bags (optional)
- pasta alphabet letters (optional)

Set, Go!

For this activity, give your child a paper plate and assorted pasta shapes. Then you can apply the glue or let your child do it. Many children can easily handle a small bottle of glue, especially when the object they are applying the glue to is fairly large.

Help your child use a craft stick to spread the glue on the plate. Then let her make designs by sticking the pasta on the glue.

After your child has made a wonderful pasta plate decoration, allow the glue to dry thoroughly. Then punch a hole close to the rim of the paper plate. Thread a piece of ribbon through the hole and tie it to make a loop. Use the loop of ribbon to hang the decoration.

Remember!

Let the plate dry overnight. Nothing is more upsetting to a child than having the pasta decorations fall off.

Make colored pasta by placing some pasta and a few drops of food coloring in a reclosable plastic bag. Shake the bag until the pasta is completely colored. Place the colored pasta on paper plates to dry overnight.

Your child can create Pasta Plates as often as she likes. Vary the colors and shapes of the pasta, or use pasta alphabet letters.

Coffee Can Drum

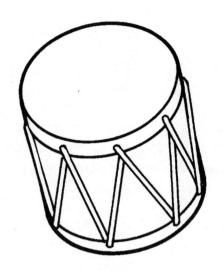

Musical Sounds

Boom! Boom! Boom!
Goes the drum, drum, drum!

Twang! Twang! Twang!
Goes the guitar strum!

Toot! Toot! Toot!
Goes the flute, flute, flute!

La! La! La!
Goes the lovely lute!

Crash — Bang!
Goes the cymbal

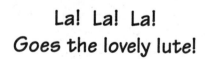

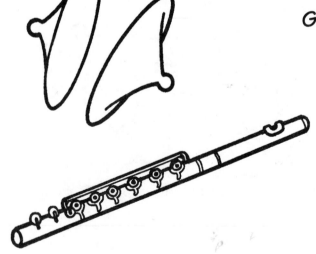

Coffee Can Drum

You will need:

- large coffee can with plastic lid
- construction paper, torn into pieces
- non-toxic glue
- craft stick
- stiff paintbrush (optional)

Set, Go!

Give your child a clean coffee can with a plastic lid on it.

Have him tear sheets of construction paper into small pieces.

Then help him use a craft stick to spread glue on part of the can's surface. Tell your child to stick the small pieces of construction paper on the glue. Continue in this manner until the entire can is covered.

Let the glue dry. Then invite your child to beat the drum!

Remember!

Let the glue dry thoroughly before playing the drum. To give the drum a shiny look, you can use a stiff paintbrush to put a light coating of glue over the construction paper covering the coffee can.

Sing songs together or play cassette tapes of music, and let your child keep time to the music with the drum.

Flower Faces

The Little Flower

There was a little flower that lived in a garden bed.
She slept so late one morning, she was such a sleepy head.
But then she heard the birds sing and the children come to play,
She heard her Mama Flower call, "Rise and greet the day!"

And so the little flower stretched her petals way up high,
She blinked her pretty eyes and smiled up at the sky.
Her mother kissed her forehead and said, "Good morning, Sugar-Pie."
And on the sleepy flower's nose, there landed a butterfly!

Flower Faces

You will need:

- non-toxic, washable markers or crayons
- paper plate
- construction paper
- safety scissors
- non-toxic glue
- pie tin or other sturdy container
- craft stick

This activity takes only a few minutes to set up and have ready for your child. Just fold construction paper into squares and cut out circles. These circles are the flower petals. They will be easy for your child to handle and glue.

Have your child glue the flower petals onto the rim of a paper plate and draw a happy flower face on the center. Some children will enjoy cutting a stem out of green construction paper. This can be glued onto the back of the paper plate.

Your child can experiment with making different kinds of flowers by cutting circles using a variety of colored construction paper. Encourage your child to make a paper flower garden.

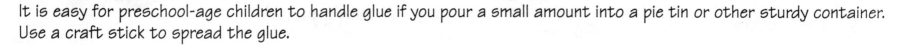

It is easy for preschool-age children to handle glue if you pour a small amount into a pie tin or other sturdy container. Use a craft stick to spread the glue.

Let your child experiment with cutting his own circle shapes using construction paper and safety scissors. However, be prepared to cut the petals for your child.

Consider spending a few minutes cutting additional circles using different colored construction paper. Keep these on hand for whenever your child wants to glue something.

Coffee Can Shaker

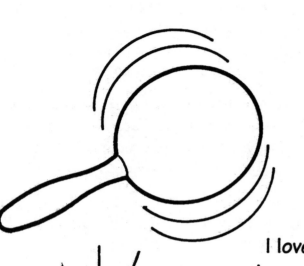

Noise

Rattle, rattle, rattle,
I love noise.
I love fireworks.
I love loud toys.
I love honking horns and barking dogs.
I even love the song of funny little frogs.

Crash, bang, boom,
I love sound.
And if I listen carefully,
I can hear it all around!
I hear trains go toot and horns go honk!
I even hear raindrops go plink, plink, plonk!

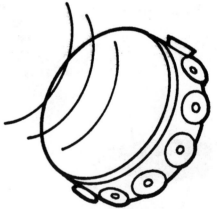

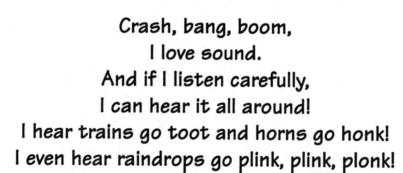

Coffee Can Shaker

Ready!

You will need:

- yogurt containers, margarine tubs, or other containers with lids (optional)
- one-pound (450 g) coffee can with plastic lid
- beans, rice, lentils, buttons, or other small hard objects
- non-toxic glue
- craft stick
- yarn
- safety scissors
- tape (optional)

Set, Go!

Have your child put beans, rice, lentils, buttons or other small hard objects into a coffee can. Cover the can with the plastic lid. Tape the lid to the can if you wish.

Provide a variety of colored yarn to glue on. Then help your child use a craft stick to spread glue on part of the can's surface and stick yarn to the glue. Continue in this manner until the entire can is covered with yarn. This can be done by winding the yarn or using small pieces. Try small pieces for younger children.

Allow the glue to dry. Then invite your child to use the shaker.

Remember!

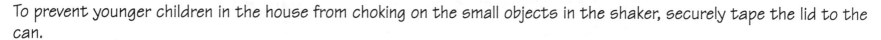

Be sure to dry the shaker thoroughly before using it.

To prevent younger children in the house from choking on the small objects in the shaker, securely tape the lid to the can.

Play music on a cassette tape or CD, and let your child shake the can to the rhythm.

To make musical shakers of different sizes and shapes, have your child experiment with a variety of containers that include lids. Yogurt containers and margarine tubs work well for this.

Pretty Pasta Jewelry

My Mommy

I have a special mommy.
I think she's pretty neat.
She gives me hugs and kisses
And she tells me that I'm sweet.

She thinks that I am special.
She likes the things I do,
So I'll give Mommy a special gift
To say, "I love you, too!"

Pretty Pasta Jewelry

You will need:

- poster paint and paintbrushes (optional)
- pasta with holes
- thin red licorice strings or shoelaces
- food coloring
- cookie sheet
- several plastic or Styrofoam bowls
- reclosable plastic bags
- o-shaped cereal (optional)

Set, Go!

Use a cookie sheet to keep the materials organized and as a place for the finished jewelry.

Place a variety of different stringable pastas in separate plastic or Styrofoam bowls.

Tie a knot in one end of a thin red licorice string, and have your child string pasta on the other end.

Tie the knotted end and the other end together for the finished piece of jewelry.

Allow your child to create additional pieces of jewelry in the same way.

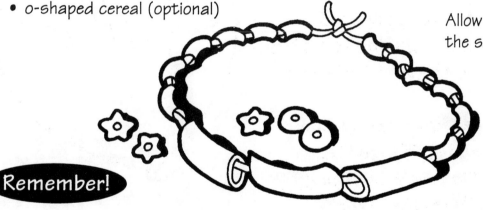

Remember!

Make colored pasta by placing some pasta and a few drops of food coloring in a reclosable plastic bag. Shake the bag until the pasta is completely colored. Place the colored pasta on the cookie sheet to dry overnight.

As an alternative, the finished jewelry can be colored using poster paint and paintbrushes. Make sure the paint is thoroughly dry before anyone wears the jewelry your child makes.

Children love giving this kind of jewelry as presents. For longer lasting jewelry, use shoelaces instead of licorice strings.

For edible jewelry, have your child use o-shaped cereal and licorice strings.

Rice and Bean Houses

My House

My house is where my family lives.
It's where we work and play.
It's where I go to sleep at night
And wake up every day!

We live here all together,
As happy as can be.
My house is where my family lives,
And it's the place for me!

Rice and Bean Houses

Ready!

You will need:

- dried rice and beans, any type
- construction paper or poster board
- non-toxic glue
- non-toxic markers or crayons
- several pie tins or other sturdy containers
- craft sticks
- plastic tablecloth
- food coloring (optional)
- reclosable plastic bags (optional)

Set, Go!

Cover the table with a plastic tablecloth before beginning to have an easier job cleaning up when you are finished.

Pour a small amount of glue into a pie tin or other sturdy container. Children can easily handle craft sticks to spread the glue. Put dry rice and beans into several additional pie tins or sturdy containers.

On a piece of construction paper or poster board draw a large, simple outline of a house for your child.

Then let your child fill in the house by gluing on rice and different kinds of beans.

Remember!

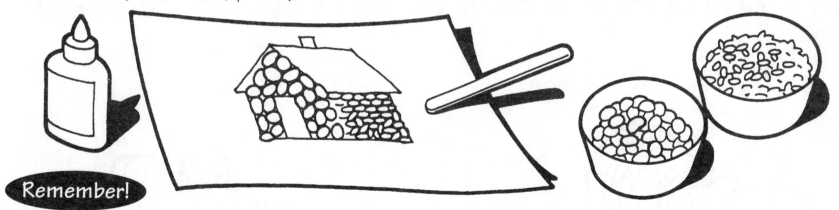

Let your child's creation dry overnight before trying to move or display it. It can be quite upsetting for a child to have his favorite picture fall apart because it is not dry.

Allow your child to experiment with colored rice. Just place some rice and a few drops of food coloring in a reclosable plastic bag. Shake the bag until the rice is completely colored. Place the colored rice in the pie tins or other containers to dry before using.

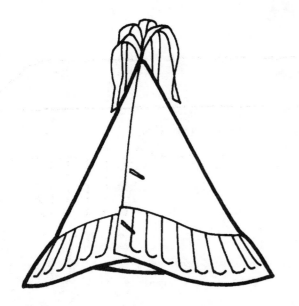

Birthday Arts and Crafts

58

"Kid Kit"

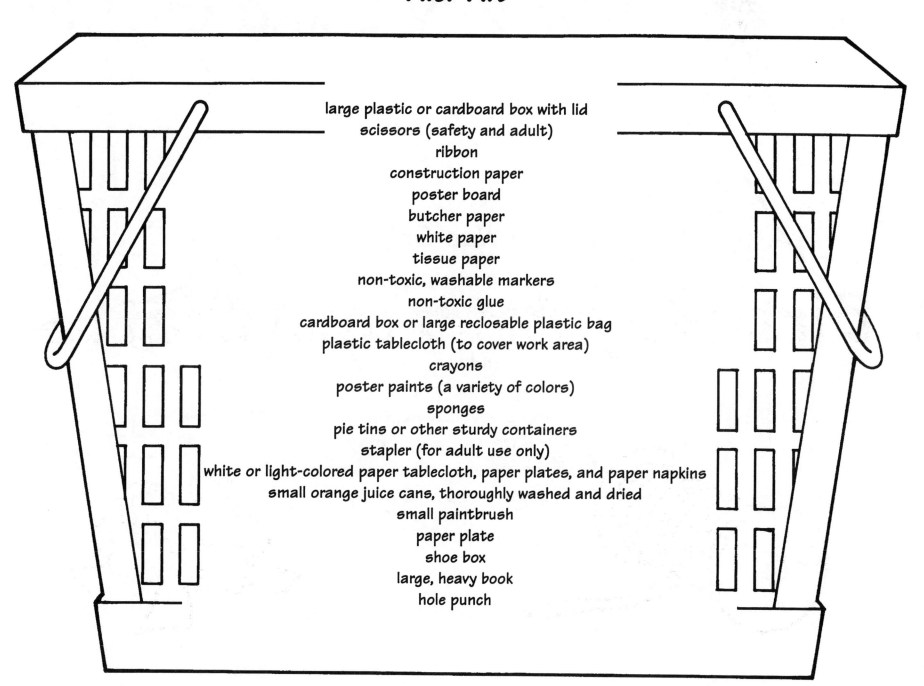

large plastic or cardboard box with lid

scissors (safety and adult)

ribbon

construction paper

poster board

butcher paper

white paper

tissue paper

non-toxic, washable markers

non-toxic glue

cardboard box or large reclosable plastic bag

plastic tablecloth (to cover work area)

crayons

poster paints (a variety of colors)

sponges

pie tins or other sturdy containers

stapler (for adult use only)

white or light-colored paper tablecloth, paper plates, and paper napkins

small orange juice cans, thoroughly washed and dried

small paintbrush

paper plate

shoe box

large, heavy book

hole punch

Paper Birthday Cake Game

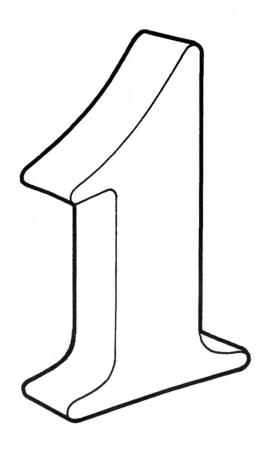

When I Was Only One!

When I was only one,
I don't remember much.
I was just a little baby.
I cried and ate and such.

And everybody held me,
And wanted me to play,
But mommy says when I was one
I slept most of the day.

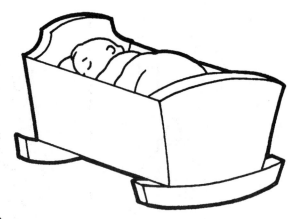

Paper Birthday Cake Game

You will need:

- construction paper
- poster board
- crayons
- non-toxic glue
- non-toxic, washable markers
- adult scissors

Precut a number of construction paper birthday candles. These can be as simple as rectangle shapes or a rectangle with a flame on top. Make a number of these for your child to color and decorate.

Draw a cake on a piece of poster board. It can be a simple outline. Your child can then color and decorate the cake using crayons.

Together, play "Pin the Candle on the Cake," a variation of "Pin the Tail on the Donkey." Use this for a birthday party game or anytime just for fun.

Remember!

If you do not want to draw the cake, just cut several strips of construction paper and let your child glue these on the poster board as layers of the cake. Then tell him to color and decorate the cake using crayons.

You might want to have children at a birthday party create their own game before they play.

Birthday Wrapping Paper

When I Was Only Two!

When I was only two,
I was a lot of fun.
My daddy says I always
Kept my family on the run.

And everybody chased me,
'Cause I tried to run away,
But since I was so little,
They could always make me stay!

Birthday Wrapping Paper

Ready!

You will need:

- plastic tablecloth
- poster paints (a variety of colors)
- sponges
- adult scissors
- butcher paper
- pie tins or other sturdy containers

Set, Go!

Cut sponges into number shapes, as well as star and candle shapes. Then prepare a work area by covering a table with a plastic tablecloth. Pour different colors of poster paint into separate pie tins or other sturdy containers.

Your child can dip sponges into the poster paints and then press them onto the butcher paper.

Allow the paint to dry thoroughly before using the paper to wrap gifts.

Remember!

This sponge-printed paper will not be very smooth after drying, so it might be helpful to press it under some large, heavy books before using it.

Have your child create wrapping paper for a variety of different occasions. This sponge-printed paper will make lovely wrapping for any occasion, and it will help your child feel involved in each holiday and special event.

Picture Jigsaw Puzzles

When I Was Three

When I was three, I loved to sing,
My grandma taught me how.
It made her very happy and
She had me take a bow.

Then people asked me more and more
To sing the songs I knew.
I sang and sang and sang them all;
My family sings them, too!

Picture Jigsaw Puzzles

Ready!

You will need:

- poster board
- crayons or markers
- non-toxic glue
- white paper
- large, heavy book
- adult scissors
- large reclosable plastic bag or cardboard box with lid

Set, Go!

On white paper, have your child color a picture of a family member or a family activity.

Glue the picture to a piece of poster board and press it overnight under a large, heavy book.

Then cut the picture into simple shapes to make a jigsaw puzzle out of it.

Your child will have a new game he can play with again and again. He will take special pride in this puzzle since it is made from his picture.

Remember!

Get a cardboard box or large reclosable plastic bag to store the puzzle. If you use a box, let your child decorate it using crayons or markers.

Your child can make a variety of puzzles about what he did when he was three by using the pictures he draws.

These puzzles make wonderful birthday gifts or party favors that children can play with at a table.

Paper Plate Hat

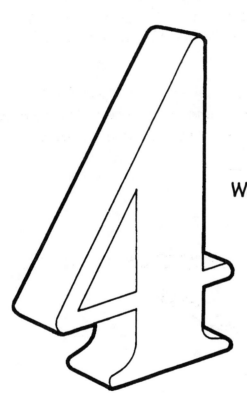

When I Was Four

When I was four, I played with friends
Inside my own backyard.
We bounced our balls and played with sand,
And rode bikes long and hard.

When we were all done playing
We would have a snack and rest.
And then we'd go to my friend's house,
Where I would be the guest!

Paper Plate Hat

You will need:

- paper plate
- crayons or markers
- ribbon
- stapler (for adult use only)
- adult scissors
- hole punch
- poster paint (optional)

This is a simple hat-making activity that your child will enjoy. Have your child decorate a paper plate using crayons or markers. (If you prefer, your child can use poster paint to decorate the paper plate. However, it is much simpler and faster for her to use crayons or markers.)

Twist the plate into a cone shape and staple in place. Staple pieces of ribbon to opposite sides of the cone, and your child has a darling hat that is ready to wear.

Remember!

This can also be done with any kind of sturdy paper you have on hand. It is also possible to attach ribbons like streamers to the top of the hat.

The part of the process that you will have to actively participate in should take a few minutes to perform.

Punch two holes on opposite sides near the edge of the hat. Cut two long pieces of ribbon. Tie one end of each piece of ribbon to a hole in the hat. Place the hat on your child's head. Tie the ribbon pieces under your child's chin so the hat will not fall off.

Birthday Plates, Tablecloth, and Napkins

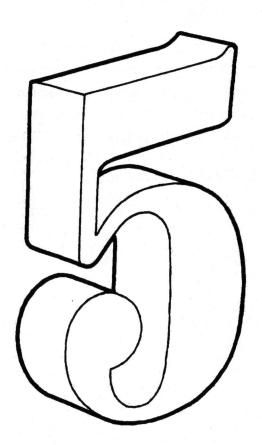

When I Was Five

When I was five I went to school
To learn my ABC's.
I loved to go five days a week,
'Cause learning's fun to me!

I learned to share and to be nice;
I made a lot of friends.
And now each day I just can't wait
For school to start again!

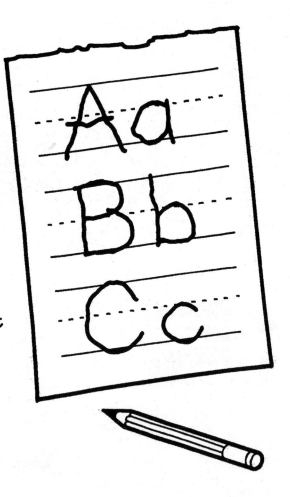

Birthday Plates, Tablecloth, and Napkins

Ready!

You will need:

- white or light-colored paper tablecloth, paper plates, and paper napkins
- markers
- construction paper
- non-toxic glue
- safety scissors
- crayons

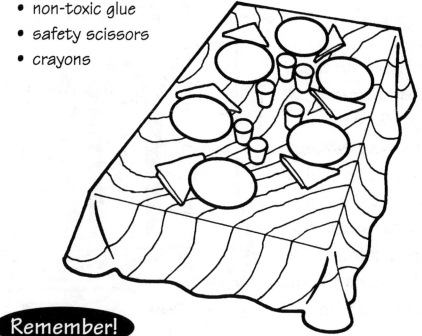

Set, Go!

This is a wonderful way to let your child be really involved with his own birthday celebration, or that of any family member, while giving him an exciting art experience that is actually useful.

Buy white or light colored paper napkins, paper tablecloth, and paper plates. Then give your child markers to draw on the napkins. Use crayons to decorate the paper plate borders, and construction paper, safety scissors, and glue to add shapes to the tablecloth. If you wish, forego the construction paper, scissors, and glue and have your child use crayons to color the paper tablecloth.

After the party supplies are complete, have the party and enjoy using them.

Remember!

Your child will be very proud of his birthday party decorations. Give him an opportunity to share this accomplishment with the rest of the family.

Have a group of birthday guests take part in their own party-making fun by having the childern design the napkins, tablecloth, and paper plates as the opening game for a birthday party. Save yourself some time and hassle, while making a hit!

Shoe Box Mailbox

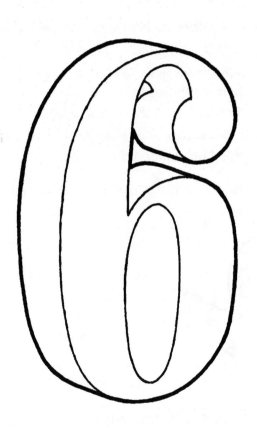

When I Was Six

When I was six I learned to read.
I was so proud of me.
It took much longer
Than it did to learn my ABC's.

And now my mother takes me
To the library to read.
There's a section there for children
With all the books I need.

Shoe Box Mailbox

Ready!

You will need:

- shoe box
- non-toxic glue
- construction paper
- safety scissors
- adult scissors
- markers

Set, Go!

Set up a work area where your child can glue, cut, and color.

Provide your child with a shoe box to cover with construction paper. Allow the glue to dry. Then invite your child to use the markers to color designs on the box.

Use the adult scissors to make a slit in the center of the box lid. Place the lid on the box and your child will have a cute mailbox for birthday cards.

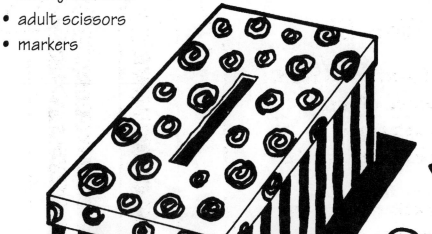

Remember!

Provide safety scissors and construction paper in a variety of colors. Let your child choose how to decorate the shoe box. There is no special way that a child must complete this mailbox and she will enjoy doing it her own way.

Tissue Paper Covered Candy Jars

When I Was Seven

Seven years old, I'm all grown up.
I am so very old.
I know just about everything
Without even being told.

At least that's what I think inside,
But Mom and Dad don't know.
They think I don't know everything.
In fact, they tell me so!

Tissue Paper Covered Candy Jars

Ready!

You will need:

- small orange juice cans, thoroughly washed and dried
- non-toxic glue
- tissue paper
- plastic tablecloth
- small paintbrush
- pie tin or other sturdy container

Set, Go!

Set up your child's work area by covering it with a plastic tablecloth. Provide tissue paper, glue, and a small orange juice can that has been thoroughly washed and dried.

Have your child tear the tissue paper into small pieces and glue these onto the can.

After the glue has dried, give your child a small paintbrush and some more glue in a pie tin or other sturdy container. Have him use the paintbrush to cover the tissue paper on the can with glue. This will harden into a sturdy shiny surface that will last longer.

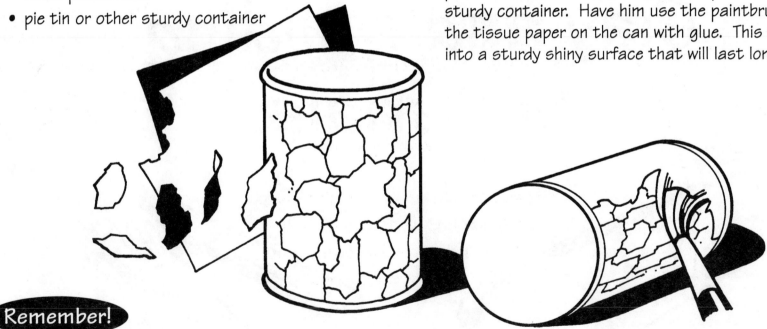

Remember!

If you are planning a birthday party for your child, save enough cans to serve as party favors for all the guests.

Let your child work on one can each day for a week or so to prepare them for the party. Then let your child choose the type of candy he would like to fill the cans with, and help him do this on the day of the party.

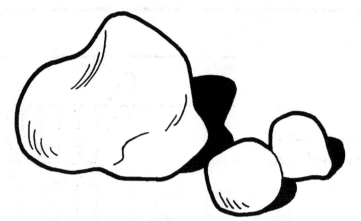

Clay and Building Materials

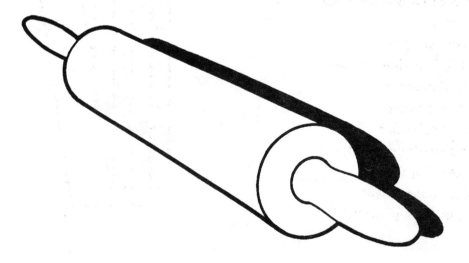

"Kid Kit"

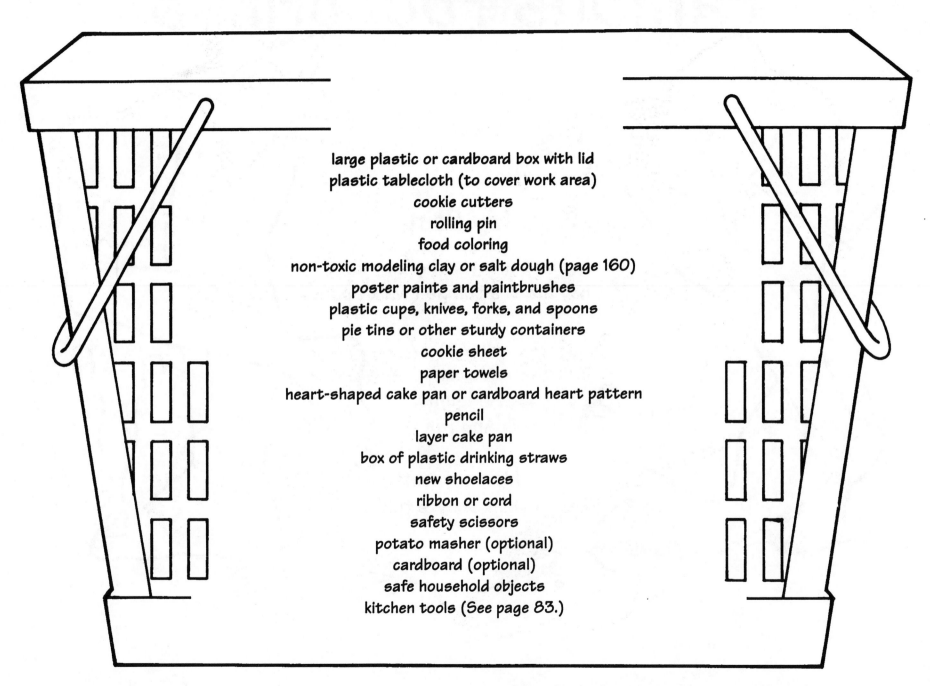

large plastic or cardboard box with lid
plastic tablecloth (to cover work area)
cookie cutters
rolling pin
food coloring
non-toxic modeling clay or salt dough (page 160)
poster paints and paintbrushes
plastic cups, knives, forks, and spoons
pie tins or other sturdy containers
cookie sheet
paper towels
heart-shaped cake pan or cardboard heart pattern
pencil
layer cake pan
box of plastic drinking straws
new shoelaces
ribbon or cord
safety scissors
potato masher (optional)
cardboard (optional)
safe household objects
kitchen tools (See page 83.)

Famous Footprints

My Feet

My feet are getting very long.
They are the things I walk upon.

They walk,
And skip,
And jump,
And run.

I love my feet!
I think they're fun!

Famous Footprints

Ready!

You will need:

- cookie sheet
- paper towels
- modeling clay or salt dough (page 160)
- rolling pin
- pencil
- cookie cutters, potato masher, and other interesting objects
- plastic tablecloth

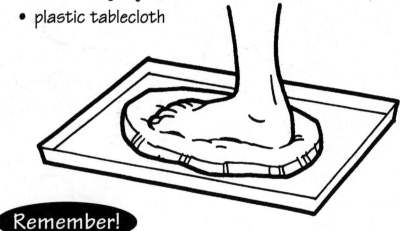

Set, Go!

Have your child fill a cookie sheet with modeling clay or salt dough.

Then put the cookie sheet on the floor and have your child step on the clay or dough to make footprints. If she does not like the results, smooth the surface with a rolling pin, and let her do it again.

Provide a variety of safe, interesting objects to press into the clay such as cookie cutters, a rolling pin, and a potato masher.

When she has finished making footprints, help your child print her name in the dough with a pencil.

Allow the clay or dough to dry. Then display your child's star footprints!

Remember!

Provide many different objects for your child to press into the clay or dough. Practically anything will work as long as it is safe for her to handle.

Use a plastic tablecloth on the table to make cleaning up easier.

Let the footprints dry for several days before moving.

Grandparents love these. Also, they are wonderful keepsakes for you of your child's preschool-size feet!

Heart-Shaped Handprints

What Are Hands For?

My hands can do so many things,
I'll list them here for you,

My hands are for holding.
My hands are for touching.
My hands are for writing.
My hands are for drawing.
My hands are for painting.
My hands are for waving.
My hands are for digging.
My hands are for picking.
My hands are for putting.
My hands are for making.
My hands are for tickling.
My hands are for clapping.

My hands are truly wonderful,
There's so much they can do!

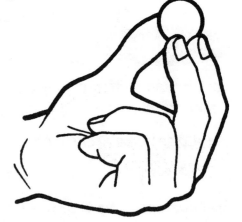

Heart-Shaped Handprints

You will need:

- plastic tablecloth
- rolling pin
- heart-shaped cake pan or cardboard heart pattern
- plastic knife
- modeling clay or salt dough (page 160)
- poster paints and paintbrushes
- pencil
- cookie sheet

Set, Go!

If you decide to purchase a heart-shaped cake pan, it will be something you use again and again for art projects and cakes. However, you can just as easily cut a heart-shaped pattern out of cardboard. Your child will probably be able to press the clay or dough into a mold, but you may have to assist him with cutting a heart using a cardboard pattern.

Give your child a rolling pin, let him roll out the clay or dough, and press handprints into it.

Use a pencil to help your child write his name by the handprints.

Let the heart dry in the mold or cut out the heart shape using a cardboard pattern and place it on a cookie sheet to dry.

Ask your child to use poster paints to decorate the Heart-Shaped Handprints.

Allow the paint to dry. Then wrap the handprints, and invite your child to give his creation away as a gift.

Remember!

This makes an excellent gift for grandparents. Have your child make more than one and let him give them as holiday gifts.

Clay or Dough Shapes

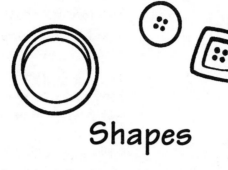

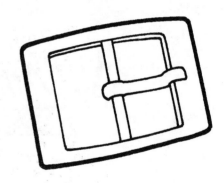

Shapes

Look around you and you'll see
So many shapes, it's true—
Like circles, triangles, and squares,
And many more shapes, too!

Hearts and stars and retangles
I've only named a few.
Now see how many you can find.
It's really up to you!

Clay or Dough Shapes

You will need:

- modeling clay or salt dough (page 160)
- cookie cutters
- rolling pin
- plastic cups, forks, knives, and spoons
- cookie sheet
- plastic tablecloth
- safe household objects

Set, Go!

This shape-making activity is totally self-directed. Just set up the area you would like your child to use. Cover the table or work area with a plastic tablecloth. This will make it easy for your child to use the clay and rolling pin. Provide the clay or dough.

Look around your house for interesting, safe objects that can be used as molds or pressed into the clay or dough to make patterns and shapes. Examples include cookie cutters, plastic cups, plastic utensils, and small toys.

Place the finished objects, shapes, and imprints your child would like to keep on a cookie sheet. Allow them to dry.

As your child tries the objects that you have set out, add some new ones or take the ones away that are not enjoyed or are too frustrating for her to use.

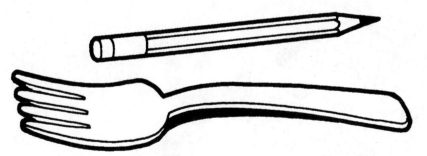

Remember!

You will be surprised how many objects you already have in your house that can be used for dough or clay play.

Be aware of the things you buy and the packaging materials. Craft supplies, office supplies, and other things can easily be transformed into clay or dough tools.

Clay or Dough Bakery

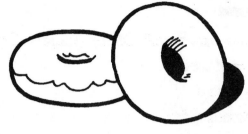

The Bakery

A cookie, a pie,
A cream puff, a cake.
These are some of the things
That a baker might bake.

A baker bakes bread,
Fresh and hot, warm and yummy.
I love bread with butter;
It's nice in my tummy.

A bakery is
Such a wonderful place,
All the tasty fresh foods
Put a smile on my face!

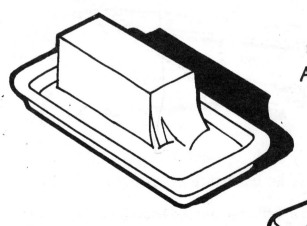

Clay or Dough Bakery

You will need:

- modeling clay or salt dough (page 160)
- rolling pin
- kitchen tools
- layer cake pan
- pie tins or other sturdy containers
- plastic tablecloth
- cookie sheet

Set, Go!

Set up an imaginary bakery by covering the table with a plastic cloth and providing your young baker with a variety of interesting kitchen tools to create clay or salt dough cakes, pies, and cookies.

Use a cookie sheet to dry the clay or salt dough food that your child wants to keep.

Invite your child to have a luncheon or tea party with a doll or teddy bear using the "baked goods" your child has made.

Remember!

Carefully check the items you use from your kitchen to be sure they are safe for your child to handle.

It is a good idea to use kitchen items that are old or easily replaced in the event that something is damaged or destroyed.

Beautiful Beads

My Imagination

With my imagination
I can see
Wonderful things
I want to be.

I can pretend
What I want to be
Because my imagination
Belongs to me!

Beautiful Beads

You will need:

- modeling clay or salt dough (page 160)
- cookie sheet
- box of plastic drinking straws
- poster paints and paintbrushes
- pie tins or other sturdy containers
- new shoelaces

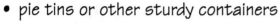

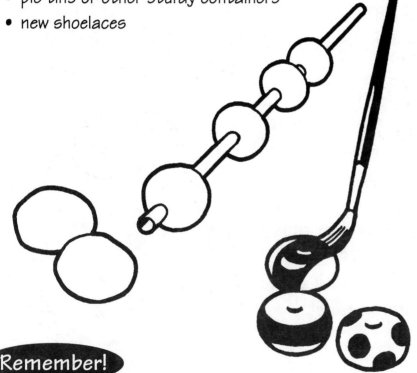

Set, Go!

These beads are so simple that many young children can make them without any help. Just provide plastic drinking straws and clay or dough. Then show your child how to roll a piece of clay or dough into a ball and push it onto a straw. After the clay or dough dries, the beads will be easy to remove from the straw and string.

After the beads are dry your child may wish to use her imagination to paint them in a variety of designs and colors. If this is the case, allow enough time for the paint to dry before your child attempts to string the beads.

Tie a knot in one end of a new shoelace. Then have your child use the shoelace to string the beads. The plastic end of the shoelace will make it easier for your child to do this. Tie the two ends of the shoelace in a knot and the beads are ready to wear.

Remember!

Make sure after each step that the beads are thoroughly dry.

Have a number of shoelaces on hand so your child can make several necklaces. These make wonderful presents.

Dough Faces

Faces

There are many kinds of faces
In this great big world of ours.
Each person has a different face,
As different as the flowers.

Our faces smile and sometimes cry,
Some laugh and some will frown.
And some are dark and some are light,
They're yellow, red, or brown.

It's true that in this world of ours,
Each has a different face,
But even though we're not the same,
We're of the human race!

Dough Faces

Ready!

You will need:

- modeling clay or salt dough (page 160)
- food coloring
- cookie sheet
- plastic tablecloth
- rolling pin
- round cookie cutter or plastic cup
- poster paints and paintbrushes
- pie tins or other sturdy containers
- pencil
- ribbon or cord
- safety scissors

Set, Go!

Have your child use a rolling pin to flatten some modeling clay or salt dough. Show him how to cut out circles using a cookie cutter or the top of a plastic cup.

Then have your child use each circle to make a face by adding clay or dough for the eyes, nose, and mouth.

Pour several colors of poster paint into pie tins or containers. After the clay or dough faces dry, ask your child to paint them using poster paints.

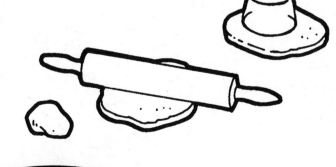

Remember!

These clay or dough faces can be used as colorful ornaments. Just poke a hole in the top of the face before it dries. After it has dried, string a piece of ribbon or cord through the hole and hang it up.

Clay Snakes

Little Snake

Little snake, little snake
In the grass,
With shining eyes,
He slithers passed.

Little snake, little snake
Sheds his skin,
And now he looks
Brand new again!

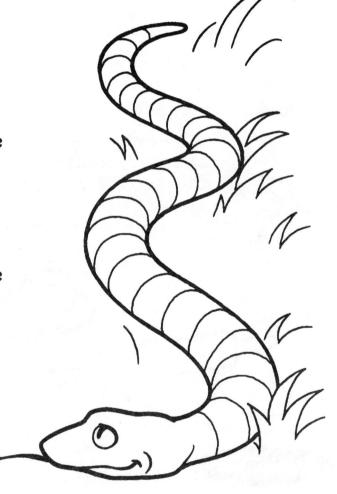

Clay Snakes

You will need:

- modeling clay or salt dough (page 160)
- plastic tablecloth
- poster paints and paintbrushes
- pie tins or other sturdy containers
- cookie sheet or cardboard

Cover the table with a plastic tablecloth, and set up your child's work space.

Provide modeling clay or salt dough for your child to use. Show your child how to use a piece of clay or dough to roll a snake. Your preschool child will easily master this skill and be able to make as many snakes as she desires without any trouble.

Pour several colors of poster paint into pie tins or containers. Place the snakes on a cookie sheet or piece of cardboard. Have your child use poster paints to decorate or color the snakes. If the snakes are painted before the clay has hardened, it will take one or two days for both the clay and the paint to dry.

To make this activity more interesting, take your child to a nearby public library and look at pictures of snakes in nonfiction books or encyclopedias. As an alternative, you may wish to take your child to a pet store or zoo that has live reptiles. Together, take a close-up look at snakes!

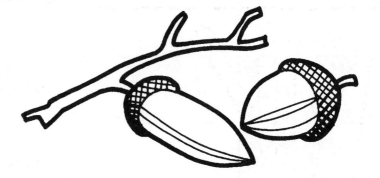

Outdoor Arts and Crafts

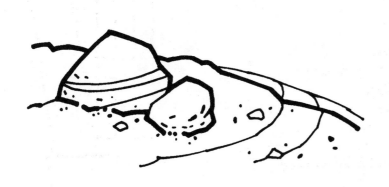

"Kid Kit"

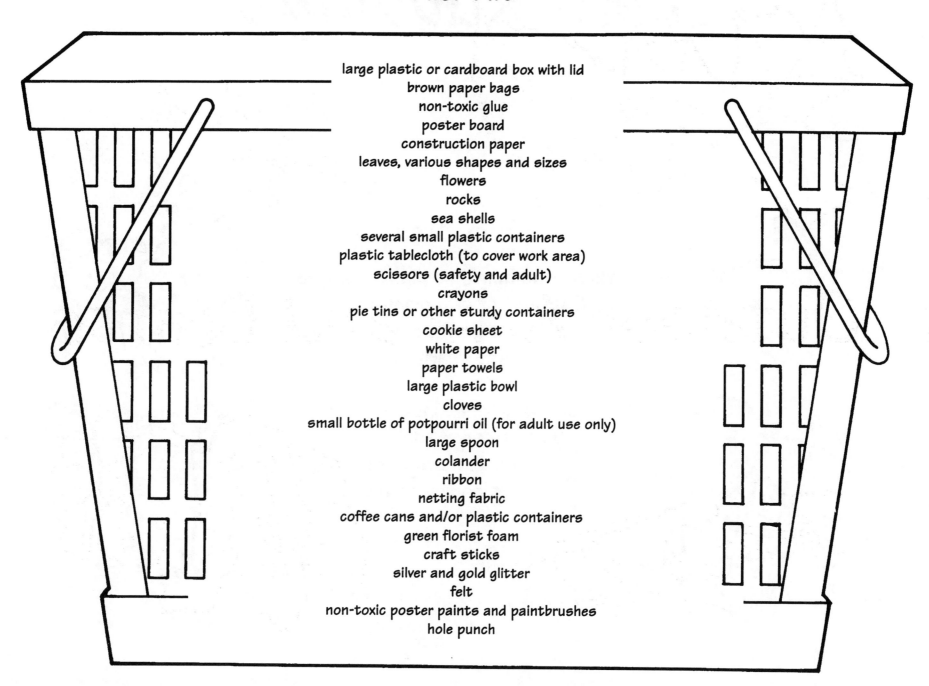

large plastic or cardboard box with lid
brown paper bags
non-toxic glue
poster board
construction paper
leaves, various shapes and sizes
flowers
rocks
sea shells
several small plastic containers
plastic tablecloth (to cover work area)
scissors (safety and adult)
crayons
pie tins or other sturdy containers
cookie sheet
white paper
paper towels
large plastic bowl
cloves
small bottle of potpourri oil (for adult use only)
large spoon
colander
ribbon
netting fabric
coffee cans and/or plastic containers
green florist foam
craft sticks
silver and gold glitter
felt
non-toxic poster paints and paintbrushes
hole punch

Leaf Rubbings

Baby Tree

When I was small, we planted a tree
Outside our own front door.
We watched it grow so big and tall
'Til I was nearly four.

Now every time I look outside
It really seems to me,
That tiny tree has grown so much,
It's just as tall as me!

Leaf Rubbings

Ready!

You will need:

- non-toxic glue
- poster board
- leaves, various shapes and sizes
- white paper
- crayons with the labels removed
- large, heavy book
- paper towels
- safety scissors (optional)

Set, Go!

The day before doing this activity, ask your child to gather leaves from your yard, the neighborhood, or a nearby park. Ask him to get leaves that he thinks are especially pretty or interesting. Press the leaves under a large, heavy book to make them easier to rub.

As an alternative to rubbing actual leaves, and as a way of making the process easier for little hands, use glue to draw pictures of simple leaves on the poster board. Allow the glue to dry overnight. These leaf pictures can be rubbed just like real leaves and will be far easier for a preschool child than holding a leaf while trying to do a rubbing.

Show your child how to place a piece of white paper over the real leaf or the glue "leaf" and use the side of a crayon to rub over the surface. Let your child experiment with different colored crayons.

Remember!

Be aware of any dangerous plants in your area such as poison ivy, poison oak, or poison sumac. Make sure your child does not gather leaves from these plants.

For an extra activity, provide your child with safety scissors to cut out the leaf rubbings after they are finished.

93

Potpourri

The Flower Bed

Roses and daisies and daffodils,
All in a flower bed.
All of the colors in the world,
Right here in my flower bed.

Every morning I look and I see,
The yellow and white and red
Of, roses and daisies and daffodils,
All in a flower bed!

Potpourri

You will need:

- large plastic bowl
- several small plastic containers
- brown paper bag
- flower petals
- cloves
- small bottle potpourri oil
- large spoon
- cookie sheet
- colander
- netting fabric
- ribbon
- safety scissors

Cover your child's workspace with a plastic tablecloth. Set out several empty, clean coffee cans or plastic containers. Tell your child to pick one of them to use as a vase. You may wish to have your child use construction paper, safety scissors, and glue to decorate the outside of the vase she has chosen.

Give your child a brown paper bag and help her gather flowers from your garden, or ask your child to go with you to buy some from a local supermarket, garden shop, or florist. If you use roses, cut just below the flower, without any of the stem, to completely avoid the thorns.

Put the flowers in a colander and rinse them with cold water. Then drain them thoroughly.

Have your child pick all of the petals off each flower and place them on a cookie sheet to dry for about a day. If your child cannot wait, you may wish to proceed without letting the petals dry. However, if you use the moist petals you may have to throw out the potpourri after you have had it awhile.

Put the petals in a large plastic bowl, and add a drop of any potpourri oil. Mix the two with a large spoon. **Note:** You do not have to use the potpourri oil if you prefer a natural, softer smell.

Cut squares of netting fabric for your child. Have your child place spoonfuls of potpourri inside, and tie each netting square with a piece of ribbon.

If you choose to use the flower oil, make sure an adult stores it in a safe place away from young and inquisitive children.

Flower Arrangement Centerpiece

In My Backyard

I have a swing in my backyard,
And a sandy place to play.
I have a place to ride my trike,
I do it every day.

I have some grass for somersaults,
And a hose for taking a drink.
Out my backdoor, in my backyard,
I have everything, I think!

Flower Arrangement Centerpiece

You will need:

- plastic tablecloth
- brown paper bag
- safety scissors
- plastic bowl or colander
- water
- flowers
- coffee cans and/or plastic containers
- construction paper
- non-toxic glue
- green florist foam (optional)

Set, Go!

Give your child a brown paper bag and help him gather flowers from your backyard garden, or ask your child to go with you to buy some from a local supermarket, garden shop, or florist. You may prefer to use artificial flowers from a craft store since they will last longer and can be rearranged as often as your preschooler desires.

Provide a couple of options, such as a coffee can and a plastic container, for your child to use as a vase. Allow him to use construction paper, safety scissors, and glue to decorate the "vase." Have him place the green florist foam inside it. The foam will make it less frustrating for him to arrange the flowers. He will be able to arrange the flowers by himself. If you are using real flowers, tell your child to pour water into the vase. Then let him pick a place in the house to display the flowers.

Remember!

Arranged flowers make a lovely gift for relatives or friends.

Remember to have your child add greenery to the flower arrangements.

Be sure to carefully shake flowers and greenery to remove any little bugs, spiders, etc., before your child handles them.

Nature Picture

The Great Big Beautiful World

Oh, isn't it a wonderful world,
All full of beautiful things?
There are cats, and dogs, and butterflies.
There are pretty birds that sing.

There are trees and flowers, and parks and streets,
And houses, and places to play.
Oh, isn't it a wonderful world,
A wonderful world today?

98

Nature Picture

Ready!

You will need:

- plastic tablecloth
- poster board
- non-toxic glue
- pie tin or other sturdy container
- craft sticks
- several brown paper bags
- cookie sheet

Set, Go!

Give your child a brown paper bag. Help her gather natural objects such as leaves, flowers, seed pods, sticks, and small pebbles from your backyard or a nearby park. Check these to make sure there is nothing dangerous or alive before your child handles them.

After returning home, place the natural objects on a cookie sheet. Provide poster board and glue. (Place glue in a pie tin or other container and use a craft stick to apply it.) Then your child can glue the natural objects on the poster board to make an interesting and colorful nature picture.

Remember!

Try this activity at several different times during the year so your child can make seasonal pictures using the natural objects.

Talk with your child about the objects, and see how many of them she can name.

These pictures will not last forever because of the natural materials used. However, your preschooler will enjoy making these pictures more than once.

Shell Picture Frame

Blue Ocean

Blue ocean, blue ocean, oh wonderful sea!
Your waves come crashing against my knees,
And your salty spray, it tickles my face.
Blue ocean, blue ocean, a wonderful place.

Blue ocean, blue ocean, where seagulls cry,
The yellow sun sets in the evening sky,
And your ships set sail and drift away.
Blue ocean, blue ocean, a wonderful day!

Shell Picture Frame

Ready!

You will need:

- poster board
- adult scissors
- sea shells
- photographs, drawings, or paintings
- silver and gold glitter (optional)
- non-toxic glue
- pie tin or other sturdy container
- craft sticks
- hole punch
- ribbon

Set, Go!

Set up a work area for your child. Provide glue in pie tins or other sturdy containers with craft sticks for spreading the glue, square and rectangular frames cut from poster board, and sea shells.

It is possible to gather your own shells if you are lucky enough to live near a beach. However, hobby and craft stores also carry shells. They are inexpensive and easy for preschool children to handle. If you cannot get any sea shells, have your child use dry pasta or beans as an alternative.

Your child will be able to glue the shells on the poster board frame by himself. After the glue is dry, let your child put a picture, drawing, or photograph in the new frame. It is easiest to glue the picture directly into the frame, so if you use a photograph, make sure it is one that your child can keep.

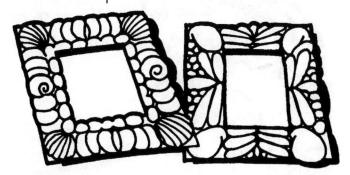

Remember!

Let the glue on the frames dry thoroughly before moving or hanging the pictures.

Make a simple hanging cord by punching two holes in the top of the frame and tying a piece of ribbon to them.

Rock Faces

Rocks

I saw a rock upon the sand.
How did it come to this great land?
If rocks could talk, what would they say?
What other children had come to play?

Were they settlers in this new land?
Or Native Americans on the sand?
If rocks could talk, what would they say?
About long-ago children who came to play?

Rock Faces

You will need:

- rocks
- brown paper bag
- felt
- non-toxic glue
- poster paints and paintbrushes
- pie tins or other sturdy containers for glue and paints
- adult scissors
- craft sticks to apply glue

Set, Go!

Take your child on a walk at the beach, in a park, or in the woods. Help her gather rocks. Hand-size rocks work best for these rock face paperweights.

Take the rocks home. Together, wash and dry them thoroughly.

Provide poster paints and paintbrushes for your child to paint faces on the rocks.

After the paint is dry, cut felt circles and glue one to the bottom of each rock to make a paperweight.

Remember!

The only portion of this activity that your child will need help with is the cutting of the felt circle for the bottom of the paperweight. You may wish to prepare these ahead of time so your child can do the activity by herself.

These rock paperweights work well, and can be used for an easy-to-make present that your child will love to give to someone!

Summer Holidays

"Kid Kit"

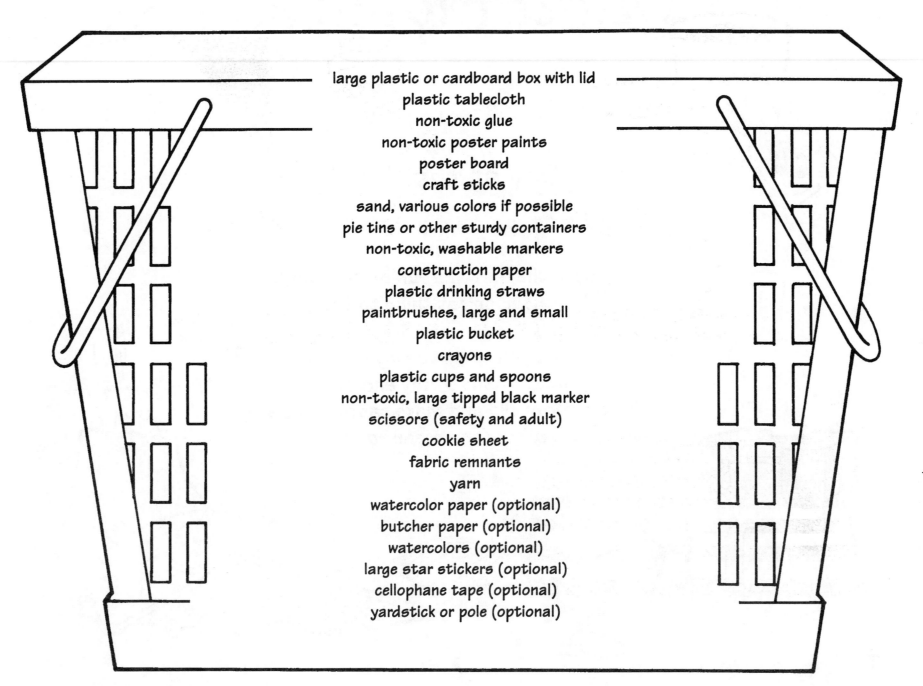

large plastic or cardboard box with lid
plastic tablecloth
non-toxic glue
non-toxic poster paints
poster board
craft sticks
sand, various colors if possible
pie tins or other sturdy containers
non-toxic, washable markers
construction paper
plastic drinking straws
paintbrushes, large and small
plastic bucket
crayons
plastic cups and spoons
non-toxic, large tipped black marker
scissors (safety and adult)
cookie sheet
fabric remnants
yarn
watercolor paper (optional)
butcher paper (optional)
watercolors (optional)
large star stickers (optional)
cellophane tape (optional)
yardstick or pole (optional)

Sand Pictures

A Day at the Beach

I'd love to spend a day at the beach,
A day by the ocean blue.
I'll play in the surf and run on the sand.
It's the happiest thing to do!

Oh, won't you come to play with me,
Today by the sandy shore?
We'll hunt for shells and make castles of sand
And hear the ocean roar!

Sand Pictures

You will need:

- construction paper
- non-toxic glue
- pie tin or other sturdy container
- markers (optional)
- sand, various colors if possible
- plastic bucket
- plastic tablecloth
- cookie sheet
- craft stick

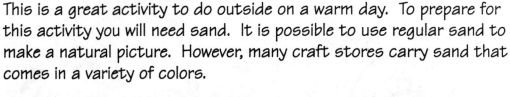

This is a great activity to do outside on a warm day. To prepare for this activity you will need sand. It is possible to use regular sand to make a natural picture. However, many craft stores carry sand that comes in a variety of colors.

Set up a work area for your child by covering a table with a plastic tablecloth. Then provide one or more small containers of sand, construction paper, glue, and markers.

If your child is using regular sand, he can color parts of his picture with markers before gluing on the sand. If he is using colored sand, the markers may not be needed.

Place your child's paper on a cookie sheet to catch any spilled sand.

Demonstrate how to spread the glue with a craft stick, pour the sand on the glue, and shake off the excess sand to see how the picture is turning out.

Let the glue dry thoroughly, and display your child's picture.

Remember!

If you are concerned about your child spilling sand inside the house, you will want to wait until you have the opportunity to do this activity outdoors.

It is easy to make your own colored sand. Add some food coloring to sand in a plastic bag. Shake thoroughly. Leave bag open for sand to dry.

Straw Paintings

Fireworks

Bright lights that sparkle;
Look at the sky.
Explosions of fire
In colors so high!

Growing and blooming
Like flowers of light.
Oh, how the fireworks
Brighten the night!

Straw Paintings

Ready!

You will need:

- plastic drinking straws
- poster paints and paintbrushes
- pie tins or other sturdy containers
- plastic cups
- water
- construction paper or watercolor paper
- plastic spoons
- plastic tablecloth

Set, Go!

Cover your child's work area with a plastic tablecloth. Provide poster paints, construction paper, plastic drinking straws, and plastic spoons. Add water to thin the poster paints so that they run easily when blown on with a straw.

Demonstrate to your child how to spoon a small amount of paint onto the center of her paper and then blow through a straw to spread the paint.

This will create a "fireworks" effect. Provide several colors of paint to make the pictures even more exciting.

Remember!

This kind of painting can also make cheery wrapping paper. Make sure it is thoroughly dried before using it.

Always use non-toxic paint to be sure that your child is not harmed if she accidentally gets some on her lips when blowing through the straw.

Dress your child in old clothes, a paint shirt, or a smock for this activity.

Water Paintings

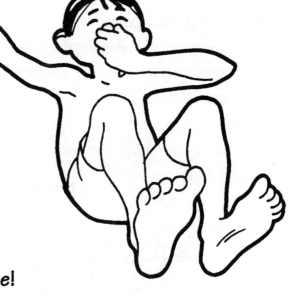

The Pool

Splish, splash, let's all jump in,
The weather is so hot.
I think we'll take a litte dip,
Let's jump in on the spot!

Hey, wait a minute, don't splash me!
Don't push me, I might fall!
And if you push me in right now,
You'll come in, one and all!

Water Paintings

You will need:

- water
- plastic bucket
- paintbrushes, large and small
- sidewalk or cement area

Set, Go!

This is a simple and clean activity for those days you would like to keep your house in order. All you need is a warm day, paintbrushes, a bucket of water, and some space for your child to paint the cement or sidewalk.

Fill a bucket with water and give your child clean paintbrushes to paint with. The paintbrushes can range from small to house painting size.

All day long, she will be able to make pictures that evaporate and have to be done again. To make the evaporation process slower, have her paint in the shade, too.

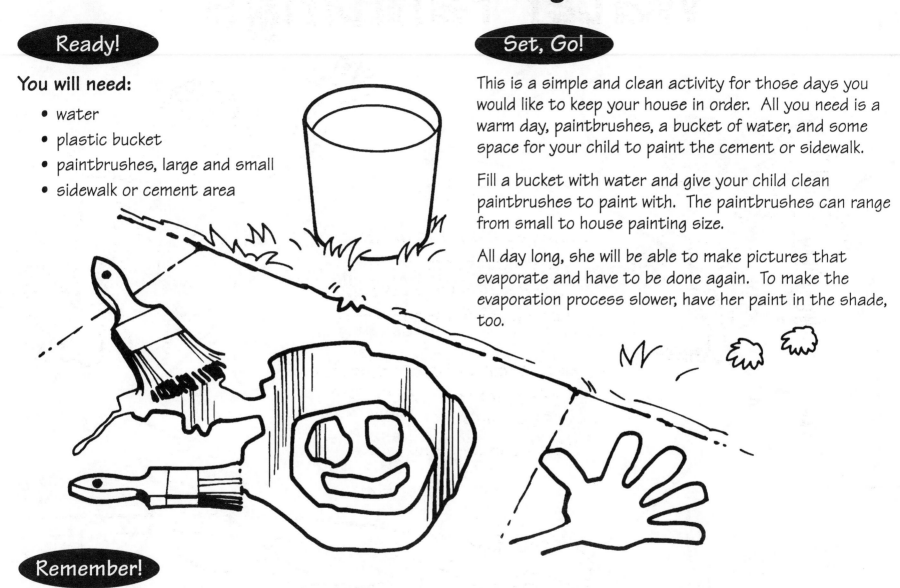

Remember!

Very young children love this activity, and it gives them a chance to be artistic as well as develop their fine-motor coordination.

This is an excellent way to cool down a preschooler on a hot summer day!

Fish Painting

Fishy Fish

Fishy fish, fishy fish, swimming by,
Out in the deep blue sea.
Oh, when I stop and look at you,
Do you remember me?

I thought I saw you yesterday,
With your pretty tail and fins,
It could have been your brother though.
I think I remember him!

Fish Painting

Ready!

You will need:

- butcher paper or construction paper
- adult scissors
- poster paints or watercolors (page 160)
- paintbrushes
- plastic tablecloth
- pie tins or other sturdy containers
- cellophane tape (optional)

Set, Go!

Set up a work area for your child by covering a table with a plastic tablecloth. Then provide watercolors or poster paints and paintbrushes.

Draw and cut out a large simple fish shape for your child. You might want to make several fish in assorted sizes. Then let your child's imagination and painting ability take over.

This activity will be fun, interesting, and simple for your child. Many youngsters enjoy making an entire school of fish.

Remember!

Let the fish dry thoroughly before displaying them.

Let your child tape them to a window to create his own underwater display.

Tie the fish to a stick for instant fish flags that will look festive and wave in the breeze.

Coloring Flag

Old Glory

Old Glory, Old Glory, the red, white, and blue.
The flag of our nation strong!
Let's stand for the anthem, and cover our hearts.
Please join me, let's all sing along.

Today is the day, that our country was born,
So set off the fireworks, blow on the horns.
Old Glory, Old Glory, the red, white, and blue.
The flag of our nation strong!

114

Coloring Flag

- poster board
- large tipped black marker
- crayons
- large star stickers (optional)
- yardstick or pole (optional)

On a large piece of poster board, make a large outline drawing of the American flag, showing the lines for stripes and the area for stars.

Then show your preschooler a color picture of an American flag, and let her use crayons to color the outline drawing that you have made.

You might want to provide large star stickers for the star section of the flag.

Allow your child to pick a place to display her flag.

Look at pictures of flags in an encyclopedia. Give your child construction paper and crayons to create her own special flags.

Attach these to a yardstick or pole and display them.

Summer Clothes
Dress-Up Dolls

Summertime

Oh, how I love the summer,
The sun in the sky so blue.
To lie in the grass on a warm summer day
Is the most pleasant thing to do.

Oh, how I love the winter,
The fall and springtime, too.
But, if I could pick one season,
I am sure that summer would do.

Summer Clothes Dress-Up Dolls

You will need:

- poster board
- markers
- adult scissors
- crayons
- non-toxic glue
- safety scissors
- construction paper
- fabric remnants
- yarn

Set up a cutting, drawing, and gluing work area for your child. Provide a large paper doll with no details on it.

Then let your child draw the face and dress the doll with summer clothes. Add to the fun by providing fabric remnants, yarn, and other things that will make the doll clothes more interesting to make.

Make several doll cut-outs so your child can create an entire family.

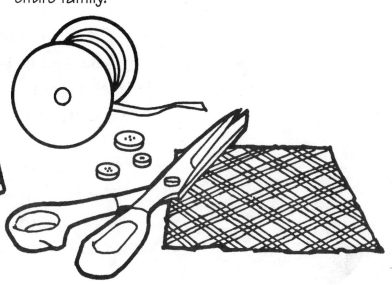

Remember!

Cut a number of these large paper dolls to use anytime your child wants to make a new one.

Suggest that your child make a doll of a family member as a special surprise or to give as a present!

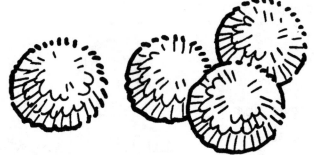

Fall Holidays

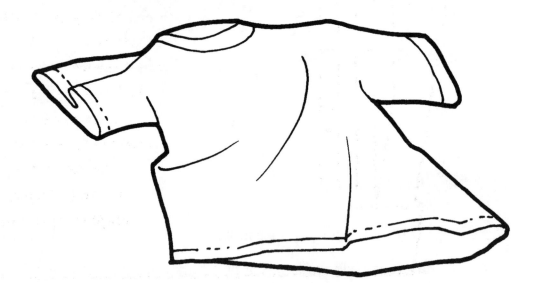

"Kid Kit"

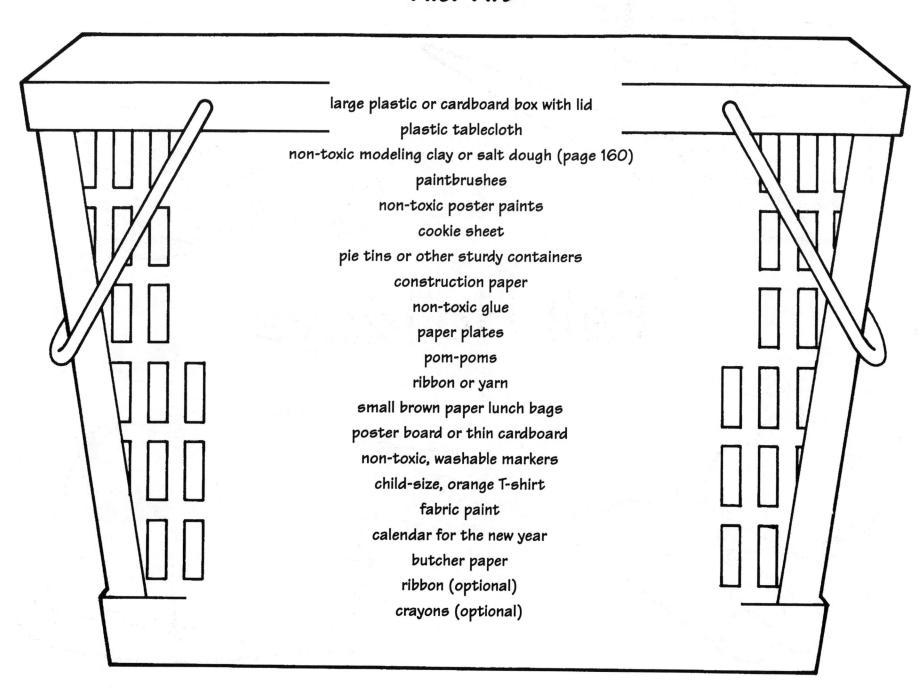

large plastic or cardboard box with lid

plastic tablecloth

non-toxic modeling clay or salt dough (page 160)

paintbrushes

non-toxic poster paints

cookie sheet

pie tins or other sturdy containers

construction paper

non-toxic glue

paper plates

pom-poms

ribbon or yarn

small brown paper lunch bags

poster board or thin cardboard

non-toxic, washable markers

child-size, orange T-shirt

fabric paint

calendar for the new year

butcher paper

ribbon (optional)

crayons (optional)

Clay Pumpkins

Pumpkin

Oh, I saw a big, orange pumpkin,
One harvest afternoon,
The prettiest pumpkin, I did see,
Just like a harvest moon!

Oh, I saw a big, orange pumpkin,
One harvest afternoon,
Do big and orange and saying,
"Why don't you carve me soon?"

So while my daddy's helping me,
I carved my pumpkin, Jack,
And put him on our window ledge,
To smile and I smile back!

Clay Pumpkins

Ready!

You will need:

- plastic tablecloth
- modeling clay or salt dough (page 160)
- poster paints, orange and green
- paintbrushes
- pie tins or other sturdy containers
- cookie sheet

Set, Go!

Set up a clay-play area by covering your table with a plastic tablecloth.

Provide your child with plenty of clay or salt dough (page 160), and let him make as many pumpkins as desired. A pumpkin can be made as simply as rolling a ball of clay or salt dough and putting a tiny clay stem on the top.

Then provide your child with orange poster paint and a paintbrush and let him paint the pumpkins. These can be painted when the clay or dough is still wet, but they should then be dried thoroughly.

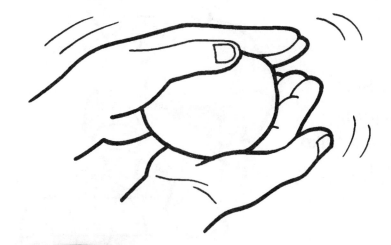
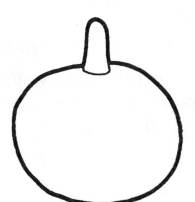

Remember!

It is important to let the pumpkins dry thoroughly before moving them.

If your child wants to paint the pumpkin stems green, let the orange paint dry first.

Halloween T-Shirt

Guess Who I Am

I have a cat who rides with me,
Upon a wooden broom.
A scary lady, old am I,
I cackle and go zoom!

(I'm a witch!)

A sailor, I am, "yo-ho-ho!"
I've got my ship and gun,
I like to loot and scare some folks,
But it is just for fun!

(I'm a pirate!)

Halloween T-Shirt

Ready!

You will need:

- child-size, orange T-shirt
- poster board or thin cardboard
- plastic tablecloth
- black fabric paint

Set, Go!

Cover your child's work area with a plastic tablecloth, and provide squeeze bottles of fabric paint.

Insert a piece of poster board or thin cardboard into an orange T-shirt that fits your child. Using an orange T-shirt will make this activity easier. However, a white T-shirt will do, or you can dye a white T-shirt orange.

Then have your child make a Jack-o'-Lantern face on the T-shirt with black fabric paint. The orange T-shirt is the pumpkin!

Remember!

If you cannot find an orange T-shirt and do not feel like dying a white one, just provide orange and black fabric paint for your child to make this Halloween T-shirt.

Especially around Halloween, black and orange fabric paint are popular colors that are readily available.

Holiday Calendars

I Can Name the Months

Twelve months for us in every year,
To laugh and work and play.
I'll name the months, twelve months for us,
And here is what I say:

January brings ice and snow,
February's for hearts,
March is when the winds will blow—
And these are just some parts!

April brings us lots of rain,
But May brings back the sun,
June brings summer, time for play—
And I have just begun!

July's for lighting up the sky,
And August's for the beach,
September finds me back in school—
And I've got more to teach!

October's Jack-o'-Lanterns shine,
November's getting colder,
December is a time for joy—
And now my list is over!

Holiday Calendars

You will need:

- calendar for the new year
- construction paper
- crayons or markers
- butcher paper
- non-toxic glue

Set, Go!

Use a real calendar covered with your child's own artwork to make an interesting calendar you will love the whole year through!

Just provide your child with construction paper cut to fit over the picture-portion of the calendar you purchase. After she uses the construction paper to make a picture for each month, simply glue these to the calendar in the appropriate place.

After all of the pictures have been glued, press the calendar under a large heavy book to flatten it. Invite your child to decide where the calendar should be displayed. Then enjoy using it throughout the year!

Remember!

Discount stores are an excellent choice for buying an inexpensive calendar to use for this activity.

Another option is to obtain a free calendar that some pharmacies and real estate companies give away around the holidays. You may wish to have your child make several calendars and give them away as presents.

Creepy Crawler

Party!

Let's have a party with all of our friends,
With ice cream and cake for fun.
We'll sing and dance and play some games,
I bet I can win at least one!

We'll pin the tail on the donkey,
Eat candy, as much as we can.
And when it's over we'll say to Mom,
"We're ready to do it again!"

Creepy Crawler

You will need:

- paper plate
- black construction paper
- non-toxic glue
- pom-poms
- black poster paint
- paintbrushes
- pie tin or other sturdy container
- adult scissors
- plastic tablecloth

Set, Go!

These creepy crawlers make excellent Halloween party decorations. Have your child make some before the party. Or, prepare enough materials so that each party guest can make a creepy crawler. Cover a table with a plastic tablecloth for your child to use. Provide black poster paint in a pie tin or other sturdy container, a paintbrush, and glue.

Prepare in advance by cutting eight strips of black construction paper for legs and providing a handful of pom-poms for the eyes, nose, and mouth of the creepy crawler.

Give your child a paper plate with the bottom side up. Ask him to paint it black. Allow the paint to dry.

After your child paints the plate which is the spider's body, then he can glue on pom-poms for its facial features. Fold and glue on the strips of black construction paper for the legs. If you desire, these strips can easily be accordion pleated for a festive look.

Let the glue dry thoroughly.

Remember!

These look adorable taped in a front window so guests are greeted by your child's "scary" artwork.

Costume Masks

The Mask

A mask is a face I can hide behind,
And no one can see who I am.
Maybe I'll look like a big, scary wolf,
Or maybe a sweet little lamb.

Then maybe I'll look like a movie star,
And you'll have to look at my eyes.
How else will you know who I really am,
While hiding behind my disguise?

Costume Masks

You will need:

- paper plate
- markers
- black construction paper
- black yarn
- adult scissors
- ribbon or yarn

Set, Go!

Provide crayons or markers, pieces of black yarn, construction paper, safety scissors, and non-toxic glue for your child to use. Cut a large, simple triangle out of black construction paper for a witch's hat, or, if capable, have your child do this.

Ask your child to draw a scary face on the back of a paper plate. Have him glue on the pieces of yarn for hair and the black triangle for the witch's hat. Suddenly your child will discover that his paper plate is a scary witch's face.

Cut eye holes and attach ribbon or yarn for ties if she wants to wear it, or hang it on a wall or window for decoration!

Remember!

Use the same mask idea for a black cat. Simply have your child add triangular ears to the plate and color it.

Paper plate masks can be something your child does on a regular basis; his imagination is the only limit!

Treat Bag

Candy!

Candy, candy, trick-or-treats,
We'll get something good to eat.

We'll dress like ghosts and leave our house.
My littlest sister will dress like a mouse.

We'll all hold hands when crossing the street,
And get trick-or-treat candy that's so good to eat!

Treat Bag

You will need:

- small brown paper lunch bags
- orange construction paper
- markers or crayons
- adult scissors
- safety scissors
- non-toxic glue

Set, Go!

Give your child brown lunch-size paper bags to decorate and plenty of crayons, construction paper, glue, and safety scissors.

Cut some orange circles ahead of time that your child can use to glue on as pumpkins.

Your child will be able to make a wonderful, interesting treat bag for Halloween.

These can be made ahead of time for parties or used for personal trick-or-treat bags.

Remember!

If you want a sturdier bag, invite your child to decorate a large brown paper bag.

As a game at a Halloween party, have children make these treat bags for their own favors. You may wish to give a prize for the scariest-looking bag.

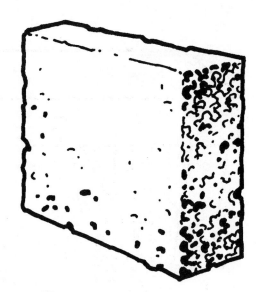

Winter Holidays

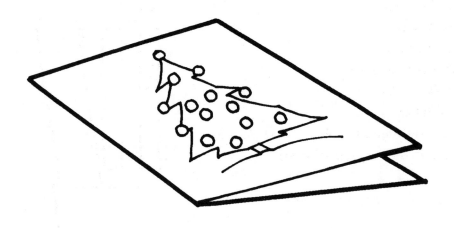

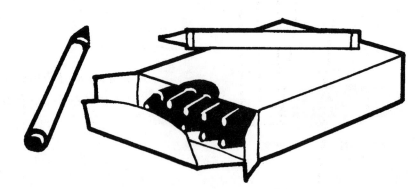

132

"Kid Kit"

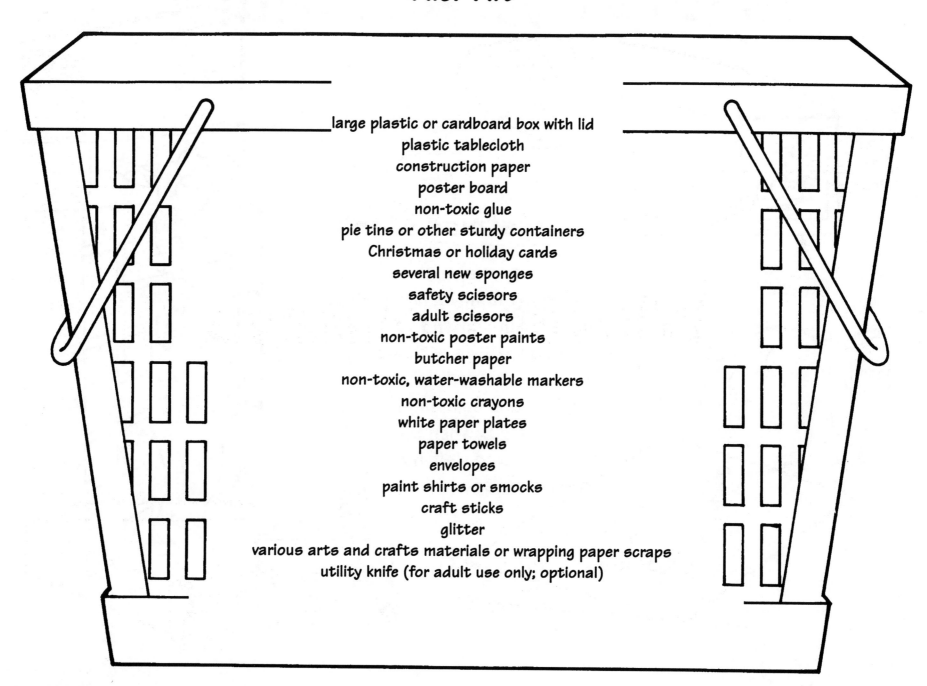

large plastic or cardboard box with lid
plastic tablecloth
construction paper
poster board
non-toxic glue
pie tins or other sturdy containers
Christmas or holiday cards
several new sponges
safety scissors
adult scissors
non-toxic poster paints
butcher paper
non-toxic, water-washable markers
non-toxic crayons
white paper plates
paper towels
envelopes
paint shirts or smocks
craft sticks
glitter
various arts and crafts materials or wrapping paper scraps
utility knife (for adult use only; optional)

Holiday Card Mural

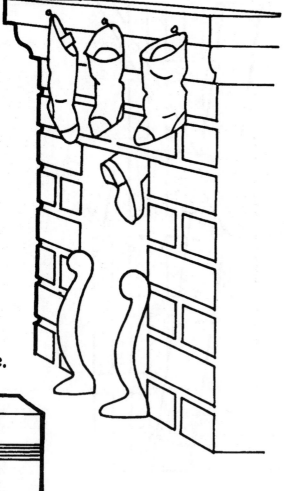

Christmas Night

On a special winter night,
I kiss my family all goodnight,
And jump in bed and try to sleep.
I'll close my eyes without a peep.

Tonight's a special night because,
It is the night when Santa Claus,
Will come and visit me, you see,
And leave me toys beneath my tree.

Holiday Card Mural

You will need:

- Christmas or holiday cards
- non-toxic glue
- poster board or a large sheet of butcher paper
- plastic tablecloth
- old clothes

Attach the poster board or butcher paper to a wall or place it on the ground or floor so it is within easy reach of your child.

Provide glue and plenty of Christmas or holiday cards. Have your child glue the cards onto the poster board or butcher paper.

After children are shown how to use the glue, they will want to do it themselves. This simple activity of gluing easy-to-handle cards on poster board will make an interesting mural that your child will be able to do by himself.

Make sure that your child is wearing old clothes and use a plastic tablecloth to protect the work surface that you use.

Remember!

Gluing is fun for preschoolers. They will glue anything, anywhere, so be sure to keep all objects and valuables out of the gluing area.

Also, you do not have to restrict your child to Christmas cards. This activity can be done with birthday cards, Easter cards, or any other kind of cards you may have on hand that are left over from a celebration.

Valentine Heart Paper

Valentine

Oh, Valentine, Valentine,
Love me true!
Oh, Valentine, Valentine,
I love you!

Oh, give me a kiss
and a hug
and say,
"I'll be your special Valentine today!"

Valentine Heart Paper

You will need:

- construction paper
- several new sponges
- adult scissors
- poster paint
- paper towels
- old clothes, paint shirts, or smocks
- plastic tablecloth
- pie tins or other sturdy containers

Set, Go!

Cut the sponges into heart shapes of different sizes.

Place a plastic tablecloth on a table, and provide pink and red poster paint in pie tins or other sturdy containers.

Demonstrate for your child how to lightly dip a sponge into the paint and stamp it on paper.

Give your child plenty of white paper and time to experiment with the Valentine prints.

Use the finished products for Valentines cards, note paper, or wrapping paper.

Remember!

Let the paper dry thoroughly.

Give your child plenty of opportunity to try different patterns and color combinations.

Wear old clothes, paint shirts, or smocks. Be sure to clear your child's work area.

Glue-It-Myself Cherry Tree

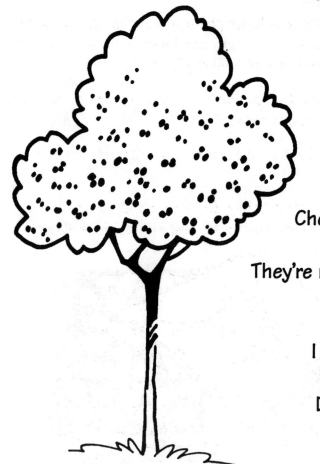

Cherries!

Cherries, cherries taste so good!
They are a tiny fruit.
They're red and round and sweet to eat —
I think they look so cute!

I love to eat them one by one
Or pick them off a tree.
Do you have a favorite fruit?
It's cherries for me!

Glue-It-Myself Cherry Tree

Ready!

You will need:

- poster board or butcher paper
- construction paper, red and green
- non-toxic glue
- craft stick
- markers or crayons
- adult scissors

Set, Go!

On poster board or a large piece of butcher paper, draw the outline of a tree. You do not have to be an artist to do this since the very simplest picture will do.

Use the construction paper to precut a large number of green leaves and cherries.

Ask your child to glue the leaves and cherries on the cherry tree.

Provide crayons or markers for your child to add details such as the bark on the trunk and the surrounding landscape.

Remember!

The total preparation time for this activity is just a few minutes.

The cherries and leaves can easily be cut without using a pattern. They do not need to be perfect to satisfy your child.

Use a pie tin or other sturdy container to hold the glue and a clean craft stick to spread it.

Allow the glue to dry thoroughly.

Experiment with different shapes for other kinds of trees, like bigger red circle shapes for apples.

Christmas Party Plates

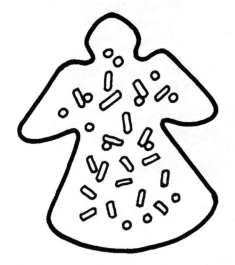

Christmas Cookies

Smell that smell?
What can it be?
We are baking cookies
Shaped liked fir trees,
And little angels, and Rudolph too.
Making cookies is fun to do!

Taste that taste?
What can it be?
We are eating cookies,
The whole family.
Munching and crunching, all day through.
Eating cookies is fun to do!

Christmas Party Plates

You will need:

- white paper plates
- non-toxic crayons

This very simple activity will make your child feel like an important part of the holiday fun and provide you with something you can really use.

Have your child decorate white paper plates with non-toxic crayons to make Christmas party plates. Because the crayons are non-toxic, the plates your child has colored can be used to serve cookies, cake, or some other Christmas party treats.

Encourage your child to make several of these plates whenever she feels like decorating some. Put these aside until you have a complete set for a party.

Use these special plates for a Christmas celebration that your child will be proud of!

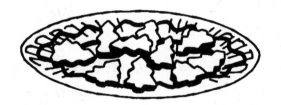

The same idea will work wonderfully for any holiday, including a child's birthday party.

Consider having a plate decorating contest at your child's birthday party with a prize for the winners. You may wish to have every child be a winner!

Another option is to let your child decorate a plain paper tablecloth for your holiday meal or for any other occasion.

Holiday Christmas Wrapping Paper

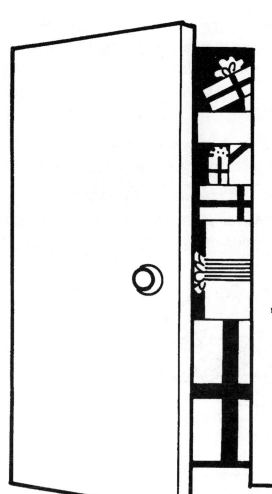

Holiday Presents

There is a special closet,
Where we must never go.
It's full of holiday presents.
We should never peek, you know!

'Cause if we did and saw the presents
With our own two eyes,
When it was time to open them,
It wouldn't be a surprise!

Holiday Christmas Wrapping Paper

Ready!

You will need:

- plastic tablecloth
- old clothes, paint shirts, or smocks
- plain white butcher paper
- potatoes or new kitchen sponges
- utility knife (for adult use only) or adult scissors
- poster paints
- pie tins or other sturdy containers
- paper towels

Set, Go!

This activity will make it easy for your child to have fun while making colorful wrapping paper for the holidays. Before you start, make sure to clear a work space and cover it with a plastic tablecloth.

Provide red and green poster paints in pie tins or other sturdy containers.

Cut potatoes or sponges into simple Christmas shapes, such as a triangle for a Christmas tree and a circle for Christmas ball ornament.

Let your child experiment by dipping the potatoes or sponges into the paint and making his own wrapping paper.

Allow the paint to dry, and use the paper to wrap holiday gifts.

Remember!

Before using this paper, you might want to let the paint dry for several days to be sure that it does not come off on the gifts.

To smooth the paper so that it is easy to use, press it under some large, heavy books.

Experiment with other colors and/or shapes for other holidays.

Holiday Greeting Cards

The Mail Carrier

The mail carrier carries mail,
Down every city street.
She stops at every single house,
And delivers holiday treats.

There are boxes from Grandma and Grandpa,
And cards from Uncle Jack.
A mail carrier is almost like Santa,
With a sack upon her back!

Holiday Greeting Cards

Ready!

You will need:

- construction paper
- markers or crayons
- non-toxic glue
- various arts and crafts materials or wrapping paper scraps
- glitter
- safety scissors
- envelopes

Set, Go!

Simply fold each piece of construction paper in half to create a card.

Have your child use a variety of Christmas colors, designs, and materials to decorate as many cards as she desires.

Allow the cards to dry.

Write a sentiment inside, or let your child help with this.

Select envelopes to fit the cards.

Decide together on a list of recipients. Then send the cards.

Remember!

This can be a great learning experience for your child and fun for the two of you to enjoy.

Your child will be able to make each card without assistance from you and really have a good feeling about her accomplishment.

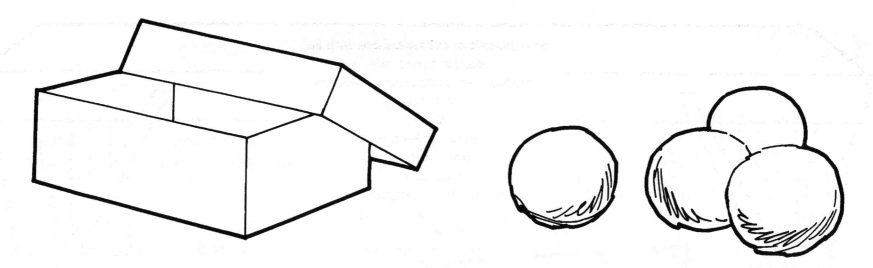

Spring Holidays

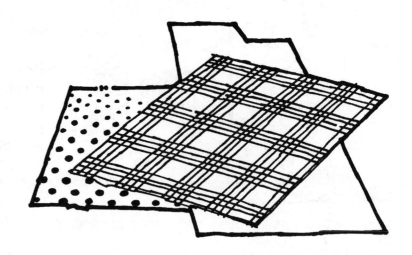

146

"Kid Kit"

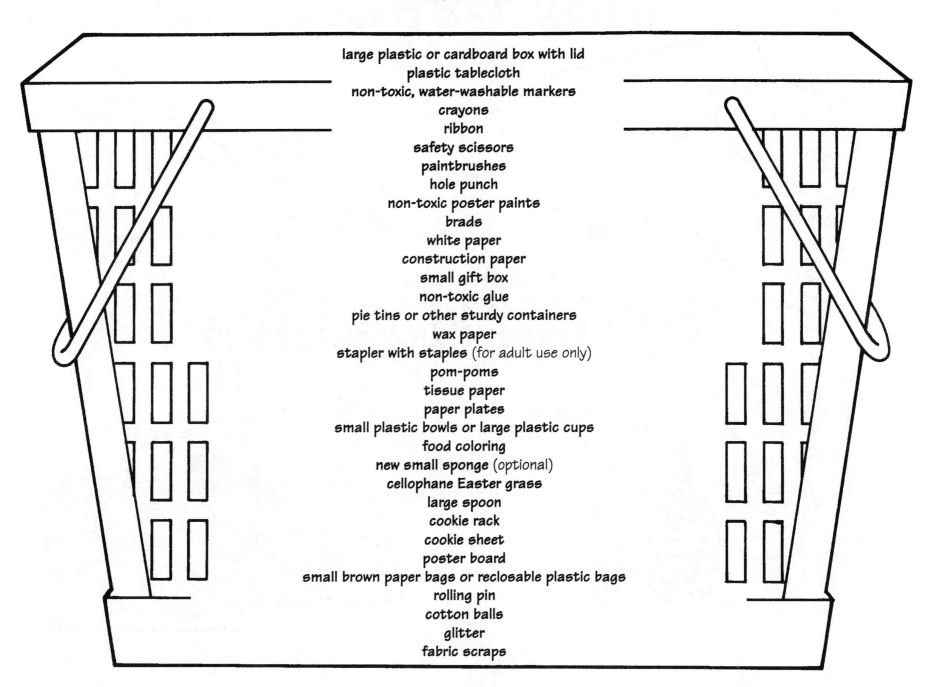

large plastic or cardboard box with lid
plastic tablecloth
non-toxic, water-washable markers
crayons
ribbon
safety scissors
paintbrushes
hole punch
non-toxic poster paints
brads
white paper
construction paper
small gift box
non-toxic glue
pie tins or other sturdy containers
wax paper
stapler with staples (for adult use only)
pom-poms
tissue paper
paper plates
small plastic bowls or large plastic cups
food coloring
new small sponge (optional)
cellophane Easter grass
large spoon
cookie rack
cookie sheet
poster board
small brown paper bags or reclosable plastic bags
rolling pin
cotton balls
glitter
fabric scraps

May Baskets

A May Basket Full of Flowers

A May basket full of flowers,
Pretty baskets full of blooms.
Our house is full of flowers;
There are flowers in every room.

There are pink and yellow and purple.
There are red and white ones, too.
Oh, our house is full of flowers,
And they smell so fragrant, too!

May Baskets

You will need:

- small gift box
- construction paper
- stapler with staples (for adult use only)
- small sponge (optional)
- wax paper
- crayons
- flowers
- ribbon
- safety scissors
- plastic tablecloth

Set, Go!

Cut a poster board handle for the gift box. Attach the handle to the box using staples. Line the box with wax paper.

Give the box to your child to decorate. Help her pick or purchase flowers. The flowers can even be dandelions from your lawn.

Then have your child fill the May Basket with the flowers.

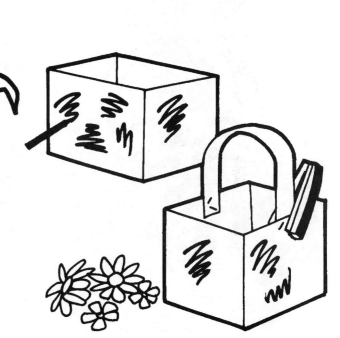

Remember!

This can be a cute centerpiece for Easter or any other celebration.

If you would like the May Basket to last longer, wet a new, small sponge and place it in the basket on top of the wax paper before your child places the flowers inside the basket.

Colored Easter Eggs

Easter Eggs

Red and yellow and pink and blue,
All in a basket of green.
Funny faces and stripes and dots,
The nicest eggs I've seen!

We accidentally cracked a couple,
Oh well, it's no one's fault.
And since it's really not much trouble,
Won't someone pass the salt?

Colored Easter Eggs

You will need:

- hard boiled eggs
- small plastic bowls or large plastic cups
- white vinegar
- food coloring
- cellophane Easter grass
- plastic tablecloth
- large spoon
- water
- cookie rack
- cookie sheet

Place a plastic tablecloth on your table to make for easy clean up in the event of spills. Mix a drop of food coloring and a tablespoon (15 mL) of white vinegar with ¾ cup (188 mL) of warm water in a small plastic bowl or a large plastic cup. Do this for each color available in a food coloring box and experiment with mixing colors.

Hard boil the eggs and allow them to cool thoroughly. Give your child crayons and have him gently make designs on the eggs. The wax from the crayons will prevent the dye from coloring those parts of the eggs.

Have your child use a large spoon to carefully lower the eggs into the dye. Help him gently turn the eggs over with the spoon. Remove the eggs from the dye and place them on a cookie rack that is placed on top of a cookie sheet. Allow the dyed eggs to drain and dry.

Display the eggs just before eating them.

Remember to keep eggs chilled so they will not spoil before you eat them.

Give your child a small basket and some cellophane Easter grass to create a darling display for the eggs.

If you prefer, have your child make a May Basket (page 149) for an Easter egg basket.

Egg Shell Pictures

The Hen

The hen lays some eggs,
The hen lays some eggs,
Cluck, cluck, cluck, cluck,
The hen lays some eggs!

The farmer brings them in,
The farmer brings them in,
Cluck, cluck, cluck, cluck,
The farmer brings them in!

We buy the eggs at the market,
We buy the eggs at the market,
Cluck, cluck, cluck, cluck,
We buy the eggs at the market!

The eggs taste so good,
The eggs taste so good,
Cluck, cluck, cluck, cluck,
The eggs taste so good!

Egg Shell Pictures

You will need:

- crushed egg shells, thoroughly cleaned and dried
- reclosable plastic bags
- small plastic bowls or large plastic cups
- food coloring
- construction paper or poster board
- non-toxic glue
- plastic tablecloth
- rolling pin

Set, Go!

To prepare for this activity, save some egg shells. Rinse them until they are completely clean. Then allow them to dry thoroughly. Create a variety of colors by placing egg shells in large reclosable plastic bags and adding a few drops of food coloring to each. Use a rolling pin to thoroughly crush the shells in the bags. Store the egg shells until you are ready for the activity.

Cover the table with a plastic tablecloth. Provide construction paper, glue, and the crushed eggshells for your child to make the pictures. Place the different colored egg shells in small plastic bowls or large plastic cups so your child can sprinkle them on her picture.

After she is finished, allow the pictures to dry thoroughly before displaying them.

Remember!

Save old parmesan cheese containers to store the egg shells. These can then be used to shake the egg shells onto the picture.

This same technique can be used to make a picture frame. Just have your child glue egg shells to the edge of a square or rectangular piece of poster board to make a festive Easter frame.

Cotton Bunnies

The Bunny Hop

Hop, hop, hop!
Let's do the bunny hop.
Let's hop around the house.
Let's do the bunny hop!

Hop, hop, hop!
Wiggle your bunny tail.
Let's hop around the garden.
Let's do the bunny hop!

Hop, hop, hop!
Let's do the bunny hop.
Let's hop, hop, hop!
Let's never, ever stop!

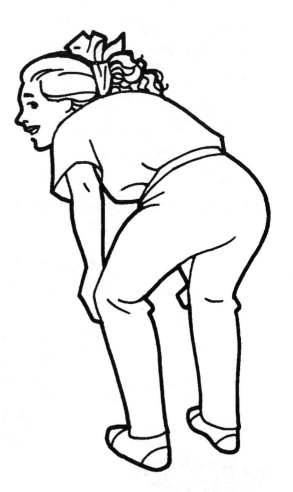

Cotton Bunnies

You will need:

- cotton balls
- paper plates
- non-toxic glue
- markers
- construction paper
- pom-poms (optional)
- safety scissors
- ribbons
- stapler with staples (for adult use only)

Set, Go!

Cut two ears out of a paper plate and staple them to another paper plate to make a bunny face.

Supply your child with cotton, glue, and markers, and let him create his own bunny face.

You can also get pom-poms from a craft store for the bunny's nose and eyes.

This cute bunny face can also be used for a mask by cutting eye holes and adding ribbons to the sides as ties.

Remember!

Let your child experiment with other kinds of animal faces.

You may wish to have your child make the faces of family members or those of favorite characters.

Kites

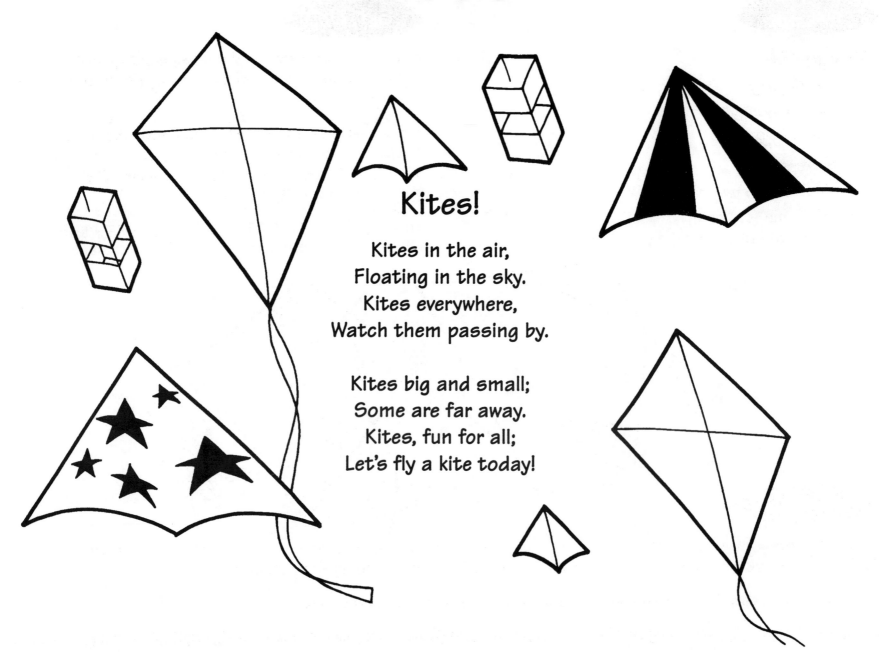

Kites!

Kites in the air,
Floating in the sky.
Kites everywhere,
Watch them passing by.

Kites big and small;
Some are far away.
Kites, fun for all;
Let's fly a kite today!

Kites

You will need:

- poster board
- construction paper
- safety scissors
- non-toxic glue
- tissue paper
- ribbon
- glitter and fabric scraps (optional)

Set, Go!

Cut several large diamond shapes out of poster board. Tell your child to pretend that these are kites and let her decorate them.

Provide glue, safety scissors, and any other materials that you have on hand, such as glitter or fabric scraps, so your child will be able to create an interesting kite.

Cut a piece of ribbon and staple it on as the tail of the kite. Ask your child to help you decide where to display the kite.

Remember!

For another interesting activity, cut geometric shapes out of construction paper for your child to use as decorations for his kite. These will provide interesting designs as well as expose your child to shapes.

These kites look cute in windows and can be made often and in a variety of sizes.

Follow up the activity by looking at the movie <u>Mary Poppins</u> (Walt Disney Home Video, 1964, 1991) or by flying a real kite!

Paper Plate Caterpillar

Caterpillar

Inching on the garden wall,
Caterpillar stops for lunch—
Munch and crunch,
Crunch and munch,
Caterpillar stops for lunch.

Spinning from a garden leaf,
Caterpillar stops to spin—
Spinning soon,
His cocoon,
Caterpillar stops to spin.

Resting in the garden light,
Caterpillar spreads his wings—
Flutter by,
Butterfly!
Caterpillar spreads his wings!

Paper Plate Caterpillar

Ready!

You will need:

- paper plates
- green poster paint
- pom-poms
- black construction paper
- pie tins or other sturdy containers
- plastic tablecloth
- paintbrushes
- adult scissors
- brads
- hole punch

Set, Go!

Set up a work area where your child can paint and glue by covering a table with a plastic tablecloth.

Have your child paint the backs of three paper plates green. After these have dried, attach them together with brads. Allow the paint to dry.

Cut caterpillar legs out of black construction paper.

Then your child can make a cute caterpillar by adding a face with pom-poms or paint and gluing on the legs.

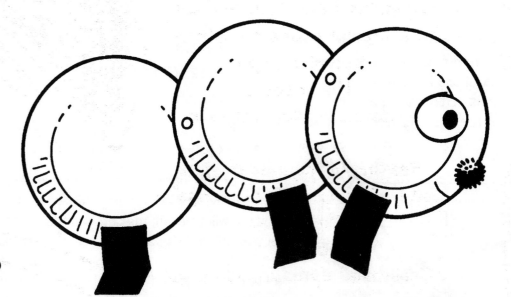

Remember!

The only step that you will need to do for your child besides setting up the work area is fastening the paper plates together with brads. This can be done before or after you cut the legs and she paints the plates.

This caterpillar can be made as long as your child wishes by adding additional painted plates.

Homemade Paint and Salt Dough Recipes

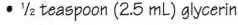

Finger Paint

You will need:

- 1 cup (250 mL) water
- ½ cup (125 mL) sugar
- 1 tablespoon (15 mL) boric acid
- 1¼ cups (315 mL) all-purpose flour
- liquid cloves
- food coloring
- microwavable bowl or double boiler

Boil 1 cup (250 mL) of water in the top of a double boiler or use a microwave oven. Add the sugar and flour, and stir. Remove the mixture from the heat. Add the boric acid and some liquid cloves to preserve the paint. Store the paint in an airtight container and keep out of reach of children.

Watercolor Paint

You will need:

- 1 teaspoon (5 mL) water
- 1 tablespoon (15 mL) vinegar
- 2 tablespoons (30 mL) baking soda
- 1 tablespoon (15 mL) corn starch

- ½ teaspoon (2.5 mL) glycerin
- food coloring
- small cup or bowl
- a few drops of liquid cloves

Mix the vinegar and baking soda in a small cup or bowl. Add the other ingredients and stir. Store the paint in an airtight container.

Salt Dough

You will need:

- ½ cup (125 mL) cornstarch
- ¾ cup (195 mL) cold water
- 1 cup (250 mL) salt
- saucepan
- spoon
- wax paper or aluminum foil

Mix all of the ingredients together in a saucepan and stir constantly over a low heat. In two to three minutes the mixture will thicken, making it difficult to stir. Place the dough on the foil or wax paper, and allow it to cool. Knead the dough until it is smooth. (**Note:** If the dough begins to dry out, add a little water.) Salt dough is a great substitute for modeling clay in many projects. After a salt dough project has been completed, allow it to air dry.